Rose Blood

Chapter of Rose Croix

I0103998

Jarrad Dickson

chipmunkapublishing
the mental health publisher

Jarrad Dickson

Published by
Chipmunkapublishing
PO Box 6872
Brentwood
Essex CM13 1ZT
United Kingdom

http://www.chipmunkapublishing.com

Chipmunkapublishing gratefully acknowledge the support of Arts Council England.

Rose Blood

1. Psychosis Turned Me into an UFO

Psychosis turned him into an UFO; he has to live, he has to live, he has two hearts, he has to live. God has the eyes of Horus and is known as Michael Mathew, the two hearted one, with aura veins and primary dark space fire hair, and he is albino, a Chinalbino, and has golden eyes and rose window sclera.

There he walks, on a moon, incarnated three-fold, three beauty queenly Kings, with breasts and naked, a rose petal penis under a pad called the Zavundular pad, with purple, gold and orange buttons to ejaculate coloured semen into beautiful woman. Rose flower nipples are on his Holy Chalice Breasts with Holy Chalice Breast Gloss. And on that moon he softly sings, lulling with his pointed tongue, "You'll be an albino soon, you'll have the eyes of Horus. Thank you for this beautiful experience." He only talks in iambic, this God of words, of poetry, of space and time, this God with all the reverence to Pandora and her holy products, her gifts from her box, for she is his muse, his Arian source, his preconception. He is a schizophrenic.

He sees Ti and Do, in a black hole meditating, or in a sun reading memory or energy vibrations, seeing its past history, and they appear in a Yin and Yang dress, the female, and in an aqua blue Astral suit. They have auras, this duo, these Holy Twins of Rose Blood, mysterious beings, of gold, silver and bronze; they have afros, black for the female Ti, white for the male Do, and have white, gothic make up and avuncular and ovuncular eyeliner, and say to him "No, Ti has to die. No, Do has to die. No, they have to die."

In all worlds of God Ti and Do exist, haunting, hovering, hating; loving, laughing, lost but not. O! And see his birth, in Nonia, where Ti and Do were cloning the race created by God in a far earlier universe; that sprung up again through twin binary pattern cellular evolution. They erected a black obelisk; turning the humans into supermen: beautiful, intelligent supermen in imitation of the blood of roses. The blood of roses is the birth and death of God, it is his life blood.

The Holy Blood is rose blood; the Holy Church is the rose; the Holy Wood is the rose petal and the Holy Spirit is the rose window sclera of God. O!

The Holy Products of Pandora are madness, witness Pandora as she came to God on the Maori Pa at Hahei, her gold flame hair bristling, answering, blowing, awake, blossoming, and her albino skin of a Chinese albino, a Chinalbino, haunting, and her tongue, pointed, singing, she has the eyes of Horus and tells him "You'll be known as Michael Mathew. Thank you, for this beautiful experience. The first fold of immortality is golden eyes; the second fold is Roseum Thornycum, the red rose seen in the mind. You've seen it and you have two folds to your immortality. The third fold is the all seeing eye, the eye of Horus, wide open eyes like the Pope who cuts his eyes open with a knife over three dead Popes under the Vatican. That is the trinity, the Eye of Horus, the red rose, Roseum Thornycum, and golden eyes, the Golden Iris."

See into his eye, at the Pa that was wide open when he witnessed the apparition of Pandora, Goddess, Arian, Aryan, The Supermodel of all the gifts of beauty: fame eyes, fame nose, fame lips, a catwalk smile, catwalk cheekbones and supermodel eyeliner and lipstick, rose petal lip gloss, orange petal teeth, an Omega top lip and an Alpha bottom lip, a rose belly button and golden eyes. See into his eye, see the thunderbolts of ancient Mycenae coming out of his pupil across his Iris, blue for Pandora, red for Zeus, purple for Hera, white for Thunderboltie and Orange for Heraclitus, God of Eye Chasm Reading, the Art of double vision in the mirror where you can meditate seeing into your third eye when your eyes are centred.

He saw the eye of Horus at the Pa in a dream and didn't die, and whoever sees the eye of Horus dies. Look into the eye of a human and see your mortality. Look into the eye of God and become an immortal in death.

There is a God that hears the voice of those who are

suicidal. Call upon the God of suicide in the summon of final fantasy, and he'll tell you what you need to do to carry on.

2. Thank You, For This Beautiful Experience

I thank you, for this beautiful experience;
I am whom had the sights and sounds of psychosis,
I am whom thought that Dilworth was an UFO
And that the principle was an arch alien
From Pluto in a body suit who ate the hearts
And brains of children from straightened circumstances.
This story is death from a brain schizophrenic
And heart only loved by a shy suicide, a
Chinese girl whom killed herself because she was pure.
    I shall have the eyes of Horace, become known
As Michael Mathew and be an albino soon.
So I thank you, for this holy experience
Which shall give me rose window sclera and two hearts
Of black so they can have body memory and beat on
Their own; and I too shall have aura veins and flame hair
Like Cynthia of Botticelli, and Rose Blood,
The supermodel who cloned Hitler in the nineteen
Thirties, and when his head was taken off and put
Into the second moon off earth and taken to
Another area of dark space where he had
Another civilisation, with Aryans, she
Destroyed it by burning it down;
All this I saw before the eighteenth of August two
Thousand and eight, when I had another breakdown
And jumped over the grave of James Dilworth, founder
Of Dilworth school for boys of straightened circumstances.
    I am the one
Who found out Cloud and Sepiroth did crash
In Roswell and whose spaceship's held at Area
51; crashed doing a space-time continuum
Plane shift. And I shall live in that Area soon.
    Our story starts with me, my life and I have to
Change the future story since I didn't become
An albino superhuman when I did hear
A voice tell me I can become an albino
Spaceship with rose window sclera and a brain heart;

Rose Blood

But there is one thing I did gain, and that is gold
Eyes, golden eyes, from a schizophrenic breakdown
But probably was from smoking the cigarettes.
    I am the Lymphic portal in the Coromandel
And I am the numbers "eleven eleven;"
Leucotomy is the white man's cannibalism,
And thank you, for this beautiful experience.
    Your mouth shall have a pointed tongue to give women
Pleasure and you shall have a rose flower penis
That is Pluto's penis, and Pandora's chakras
And holy chalice breast gloss and chalice breasts.
You shall be an immortal, 51's spaceship
And save the Greys from being cloned at 51.
You shall live forever; see new universes.

3. The Lily Blood of Rose Blood

An albino, this Rose, pale and white. With aura veins and primary red space, albino streaked flame hair, and with the height of three bodies, is of immortal race of Azrian, and Arian; and stars are seen on her earlobes, libraries, she travels into black holes of star scars, and she is white. She, whiter than the ties which bind a Cloud, whiter than Everest and with red rose flower petal teeth and with rose window sclera is purest, and is seen with a halo as her wreath. She is coming to see me, this lovely and we shall kiss and kiss. I wish, dearly.

Aura nebula, albino stars and astral dust spoke in dominant dark space, darkness still there since the beginning which was the word and was with the word; now matter, energy and time exist, and arrange themselves through the first till the tenth dimension, where all possibilities of all possible universes exist.

The grey constellation Invera sang, pulsed neutrons as it had a pulsar and pulled in asteroids with its immense gravity. To its place in space and time came an enormous human eye; it had a golden iris and thunderbolts from the pupil: white, black and red; in folds of colour of the highest Chinalbino. It was Rose Blood spaceship. Rose Blood: the supermodel who cloned Hitler in the 1930's; making a double of his body that did die, but whom, the real Hitler, had his head taken off and put in earth's second moon, that was seen in medieval times, and transported to another area of dark space where he had a civilisation of Aryans that lived off vegetation though Hitler lived off the brains and hearts of children to be immortal, for whoever eats the brains and hearts of children are immortals.

She had destroyed the civilisation of Hitler's in the Muhumagian universe and was returning to earth; she destroyed it by throwing flames from her hands. She had flew here in her spaceship that was her own eye, for she was partly cyborg, for she had seen the cyborg eye in a schizophrenic delusion, and she was a black fold cyborg, only missing one fold to be absolute.

Out of the golden eye came the very white and red haired

Rose Blood

tall chinalbino Rose Blood; an Arian, Aryan, Eleenzetrialeen and Ulzat, and also Zabuga. Her flaming hair was three times her body length and she was missing one eye, showing the chopped off stem of a rose flower; her other eye was golden, and had eleven white pupil dots around the edges. They slowly spun in circles as she took in the sight of the Invera constellation point. She was of immense height, as tall as one of the twin towers that Dilworth destroyed in 9:11, with Ti and Do flying the planes saying as they were about to crash, "No, Ti has to die in that plane," and the other "No, Do has to die in that plane," And together "No, they have to die."

She drawed a pattern on her forehead and the immense eye spaceship slowly warped to a smaller size and she held it like a magician holding the moon and placed it back onto the flower stem in her head until it spun like the other, revealing two white circles.

She then moved her arm up, pointing with her very pointed index finger and made an orange circle, a green rectangle and a blue octagon and another orange circle. A portal opened and inside it was grey or greyer than the stars of the Invera constellation and civilisation point.

A voice came of the Invera dimension itself, saying "Come, come, come...
" a Gregorian chant, that dark, heavy tone which the Dilworth trust board do around the grave of James Dilworth to evoke his spirit and have him walk around the fields of Dilworth school.

The portal enlarged and hovered, still and unsafe, a portal to the dimension of philosophy; she stood still then took a step, walking on an invisible bridge in dark space and walked through the portal into greyness, bleakness, heaviness, screeching, that of the philosophical; the scariest dimension in all the universes. Her hair set like an orange sun in the greyness like murky clouds and the portal suddenly, sharply and silently closed as the shapes she drawed slowly unfolded and fell apart, until they dissolved in outer space; cold, dark, livid outer space.

Grey, misty grey, bleak and evanescent grey shadows of

the Invera cast and threw their shapes everywhere, across the garden, in the air and on the castle. A black hole opened in the sky and threw walked a beauty queen, red hair, white skin, freckles.

Rose Blood appeared and hovered, her golden eyes blazing; her red flame hair burning, she hung in grey space. An Aryan. An Arian. An Eleenzetrialeen. A Zaon Kaon albino. She hovered in grey space and slowly flew into the castles opening door, that castle of the Invera. Huge and black, white and grey; the door black, with roses engraved on it and the head of the Medusa on the front. She held out her hand onto the door and opened it and stepped onto black and white tiles and walked. She saw the painting of eyes, they were moving.

She stepped closer to the first. It was shy she had come. To gain answers to the years she had lost of earth when she was destroying Hitler. She saw Michael Mathew moving very fast, that principle of Blood school who was really an alien from Pluto, in a body suit. She saw Pluto, blue and crystal, round and hovering in dark space of the constellation of Blakvakia. That was the name of the constellation of the solar system of earth and the holy planets and the sun.

On the floor or a gymnaesium Jarrad Dickson was bleeding from his feet, and Mr Mathew was moving very fast on the gymnaesium balcony saying "He, has to die. He has to hearts." A student asked, "Are you an alien?" He replied, pointing down at the floor, "There's a base under the school." The student asked, "There's a base?" Mathew responded, "That's right, there's a base. I am an alien, I have a spaceship. I eat hearts to live, to thrive, he has to die! Did you know we have a spaceship under the A frame, it's older than this universe. It has openings at the bottom and it's the spaceship of James Dilworth. With it we shall run the world. We already have a world goverment. I need his heart to open it, it's the key. Jarrad Dickson has the heart of James Dilworth."

And she looked at another painting, where Jarrad Dickson was in bed in Saint Josephs hostel, his pupils dilated as he was having a psychotic breakdown, hearing voices, seeing visions. Phantasmagoria, the visions of Jarrad Dickson. A voice came out of the painting, "Don't worry Jarrrraaaaaaaddddddddd....you have the heart of James Diworth. The school need it. You'll go down in history. I'm dead. I'm you when you were younger. I was in love with myself. I love you Jarrad. Don't worry. We were always meant to die. We have an IQ of 236. They're coming to get your heart now. Who will open the door?"

Rose Blood was terrified, she knew Jarrad Dickson was turning into an Arian and Aryan, an immortal with golden eyes. "I must return to earth," she spoke, "I need to return to earth, she spoke, "I have to return to earth."

She looked at another painting, she saw in the golden frame no one entering his room that night of the eighteenth of october, when he had a psychotic breakdown on the eighteenth of October in Saint Josephs. "Michael Mathew has to die," she spoke. "He's one of those blue aliens from Pluto, from the uncivilised civilisation points. Just like that alien Helen Clark, the arts dictator from New Zealand."

She moved out of the castle and walked into the garden and saw the gardener, a frail looking human, immortal for time doesn't exist here.

The gardener spoke, "So how did you destroy Hitler? What were his last words?"

Rose Blood looked at the sky and uttered, "I burned him to ashes. His last words were, "What's an albino?""

"Hollywood will slay itself, will wed itself, will impregnate itself," the gardener spoke to Lily, "And the Arian swastika will rise."

Rose spoke, "Jarrad Dickson is turning into an albino. I'm not sure if I love him, like I loved Aeneas, for I was Dido, queen of Carthage, and I am an immortal. I faked my death, but you have seen that sight, as I burned the palace down with flames from my hands in the Unverae dimension with your friend, their gardener. There are three types of albinos. The ones with no powers, which the Vatican on Earth fake by them applying make up, to hide the truth of the true gods. Second, the albinos who are hydrologists, who do hydrology, hydrologen and hydrologism; drinking over fourty cups of water a day which turns you into an albino. Such is William Butler Yeats, who was Goethe, Jesus Christ and is now Marilyn Manson, America's absinth. He hires doubles on each album, and they are all Marilyn Mansons but the true one writes the lyrics, and is he the new Homer? Was Homer blind but can now he see? I don't think so, but I was going to play Alice in his movie Phantasmagoria: The Visions of Lewis Carroll. So was Shakespeare, a hydrologist, who is Homer in the Simpsons, and created Garfield, that cartoon, and in one of his dances, you see a stream of images from South Park, which Shakespeare created, and aliens invade earth in the later series and Kenny takes of his hat and he has blonde hair. Thirdly, there are the schizoprhrenics, who see sights and sounds and that turns them into albino Gods, whether they are Zalbinos, Walbinos, Eleenzetrialeens, Ulzats or Zabugas, the highest of the high. Those are the albinos, and Jarrad Dickson is turning into the highest: a schizophrenic God with golden eyes and white, beautiful skin with rose window sclera, a roseum thornycum energy transversion shield and a scanner adjustment system to scan universes between his eyes. And millions of more powers, he will be able to read the book of absolute I predict. Thank the roses for this beautiful experience."

Rose Blood

4. I'll Call You Me, Hua Nian, if You Call Me We

The two were sitting in the meadow, kissing each other, twin brother and sister. Mathena and Sophus Underwent. Mathena leaned forward, laying a kiss with her red lips upon his forehead and he then gently fondled her breasts.

Rocking upon each other, Sophus saw her head spinning around, generating a pointed chin. It slowly began to sink down, revealing a perfect circle chin, shaped like a perfect circle, with a blue astral energy cone pointing down, he thought "she's astrogirl!"

Her eyes went from blue to gold, and they carved a perfect image. The image of a black moon with thunderbolts of different colours radiating out from it, blue, white, red, yellow, green, purple and orange; there was a golden thunderstorm behind the black moon on a blue ocean planet, the colour of her eyes before they changed. She had changed and he was changing too.

Her eye structure went from a pointed oval shape to a star shape with eight corners around each eye. She was above Santa Clause. She was a star star star star star star star star star albino. Her skin went from pasty white to albino white, the colour of a white rose, and slowly gold and yellow cream colour began to sink into it, revealing her to be an Arian.

Suddenly, like she was using telekinesis, her hair started waving in the air that had only a little wind, it was shooting up, suddenly it was in flames, of red, yellow, orange and gold; she bore the hair of an azrian and the eyes of an azrian, the highest attainment of godhood. Her legs slowly shape shifted, going from albino white to aqua blue thunderbolts and within and above her cleavage jewels encrusted allowing what is called The Holy Chalice Breasts, and soft hues of colour revealed Holy Chalice Breast Gloss.

Her hair was fire above a perfect spherical head, and he climaxed. Ejaculating into his twin sister, his love of her life. She was the White Emperor, and he was the Black Emperor. Finally they had come together. She had E face perfection and 11 white pupil dots within in a perfect circle in the outer edge

of her iris, and other irises he could see around her eyeball,
which was showing more now, because of the bone structure.

One was slime green, with no pupil, the other was arrayed
of an eclipse, the other of clouds and the other of a golden
rose with a dark halo of a black hole in the middle of it. She
was Universa to him. And he was Universus to her.

His hair was flaming also, the same colour, and he had the
same eyes, except he had no breasts. He had the exact same
proportions with the same power as hers. They were Azrians.
The highest lifeform in all the universes. Never had there
been an azrian before. She climaxed, seeing into his golden
eyes, in the whirlpool of their transformations, at the same
time he had climaxed, and she held him in her, not letting him
go, letting the ejaculate stay in the condom, since she did not
want to get pregnant on their first time.

The stars were shining bright before their eyes, as Mathena
lay her head upon Sophus's chest in the meadow, and the four
moons were all full, for it was they had come here especially
on the night of The Four Full Moons. She said, "We are
Azrians now, the highest of the highest. But we cannot forget
our love for each other, ever. We shall forever be in love.
Creating universes together in the past, since this one is the
last one, and the great war is coming as they all reincarnate.
We shall see the end of this universe, for far it will last, far
further than all the others, but we shall travel through the
unverae and unveraod dimension to other universes, other
lands, other dimensions and other times. We shall live out all
time, and then we shall become something else, an entity in
nothing, for our bodies shall survive the Big Boom that shall
end all universes. We shall remain forever after, with each
other, drinking our heart juices, watching movies in our
spaceship, and I choose the Golden Pillar of Cloud spaceship,
which hopefully you will choose with me, and forever we
shall live in that. The only two remaining. With the
destruction of all the dimensions, the universes, matter,
energy and time only us two will have the memories of life in
the universes, holy life, that has existed ever since it was
created by Me and We, and you are we, and I am me, I'll call

you Me, and you'll call me We."

Sophus aswered, "Yes, we are the two azrians, the Holy
Twins made of Holy rock, that created time and space, the
gods of negative thought that shaped the holy unverae
dimension, that helped the haratians shape the eye chasm
reading dimension, and created the first universe, the rose
universe, and shaped many others. I have seen the paintings,
and you look like her, Godeena, and I must look like him,
God, Michael Mathew, they wear those robes with florid
designs on them and shape universes by sending bolts of
lighting from their hands into planet matter. We created the
human species in our own image, and that of aliens, from the
images we saw in our younger days. Some life he did not
create, like cats, which were created by Casamus, the god of
thunderstorms, tornadoes and volcanoes, who created a
universe in zillions of years by sending bolts of lighting from
his armpits. Other gods did things different."

Mathena answered, "We will have much to answer for.
Jesus Christ has already reincarnated, and with his holy
lineage, what will he think of us? For years his family have
been seeking Me and We, the Holy Binded Twins, who also
have sex, like we just did, and it was very good, Sophus. But
they have been looking for us for aeons and aeons, for
universes and universes. And though we are white rose
cyborgs, and Jesus Christ is a black rose cyborg, he still
weilds power, influence and far great experience. He could
destroy us, and with the help of his family, those reincarnated,
or those to reincarnate further, what shall we do? Jesus Christ
is the most powerfull, but surely we can find an ally and a
friend with Scion, the other Jesus Christ, the son of the God
of the other Unverae Dimension, that of the space time bend.
For scion's father, Gott, stored his brain behind the unverae
dimension, where others are stored in the unverae dimension.
I remember that time with Scion, as he tried to handle his
great power, and he lost control of his brain, and it ended up
unstoring in many layers of brain matter in dark space in the
Arch 54th Universe, and the Muhumagians were trying to
collect it to eat it, to become smarter, taken on by a sudden

psychosis from Mathew, the dark financier that lived for billions of years by eating the brains and hearts of children, and his dark spaceship made from their organs that flew to the Holy Planet of Juppiter. Far ago that was, in the primary time of the Holy planets, where he caught an Arian, with her orange flame hair, her pale white milky skin and her six metre long body capable of entering black holes, and attempted to clone her and eat her brain repeatedly in the same body that was cloned for her IQ points, that was at the Hotel of Mist. It's a myth that is true, and he'll never reincarnate. Gone are the days of the Crucifiction of the perfect Circle, that of the organisation at the hotel, that secret society, that attempted to create a standard human population around the holy planets, wiping out the Arians, but they still wanted to become one, though Mathew never did. And he rotted in his grave. Gone are those days. Anyway they were taken over by the thought of living longer by eating Scions brain, but it all autocombusted, and they couldn't eat it. That was hard for Scion, hopefully we will never have as much trouble, for its hard to gather experience."

Sophus was thinking, after a minute, he said "But we have an Azrian Energy Transversion Shield. It allows you to be in danger safely, if you are cut or bruised, which we won't be, for our bodies are harder than wilotif, made of hebrewveteralarla and wilowtalaleena, and I mean attempted to be cut or bruised, the attackers will merely pick a gold rose, made of argentum itself, or a different object, depending on which we choose, which we can change by drawing a pattern on our forehead. Anyway, it's time to go home. I think we should shape shift to our older forms by drawing a pattern on our foreheads, and walk home, so we don't go public yet. Though we should go public at some point soon, so they know who we are. Me and We, Godeena and God, Mathena and Sophus Underwent." Saying that, he drew three triangles on his head with his long fingernail tip, that of his index finger, and slowly started to shape shift.

Small rose petals began to encircle his body, going up, down and sideways in cascades, and in all directions, slowly turning over, and they were gold rose petals, and he slowly came back to his older form. Mathena did the same, and her petals were gold also. They were gold reptilian hybrenas, who shape shift by gold rose petals moving over their bodies. A gold reptilian shape shifter, hybrena or hybrid can shapeshift in water, while he or she walks through walls or while a rose is picked from their energy transversion shield. The colour gold bears the mark of the highest power of folds, and folds are the rating of powers by marked colours.

5. The Fifth Dimension

Pandora's People suddenly appeared in the high courts.
Previously on television, the Illuminatti, Blood Film College,
were speaking about the "Dead Children of Lymphis" in the
Pa at Hahei, vats boiling their meat with oil and in marinating
buckets with pickles and tomatoes and how they were shipped
off to cannibals, the most notorious Kim Jong Il. An IQ test
appeared before he teleported and he sat doing it for one hour,
and at the end it was scored. It was 124. He said, "I passed."
Then his hand went to his heart and he said "I just had a heart
attack!" A glass of milk with chocolate in it was quickly
drunk and eaten. And he said, "Yum!"

He was paid a million dollars to say the "Peek-a-boo" on
the Peekaboo channel. He was cloned when he crashed his car
into the gymnasium. He is Pandora's People; an albino in a
black hood that is the persona of the play Pandora's People,
written in the 5th dimension by HATTILLA HATTILLA. His
play, because it was written in the 5th dimension, came to life,
and the characters, unkillable, are around the world telling
people about a party they are assembling on Miami beach and
Hahei. Everyone there will meet Ti and Do, the monkeys of
the play with their drums and have a great party. Little do
they know they will be raped, molested and will be vomiting
and trapped in a force field for five days with crashed aliens;
such as the emperor from Star Walk.

"I played Darth Cornelius in Star Walk, and I'm the son of
Darth Cornelius" spoke Pandora's People. "What's going on,"
spoke the high judge, looking like a senator from America on
television that HATTILLA HATTILLA saw on TV in a
mental health ward, where he nearly killed himself because he
thought that they hypnotised him to think that an actress will
be executed if he didn't kill himself because he is an albino.
He was going to jump off the bridge, but then they closed the
door after he put his shoes on.

"Before I summon the souls of Ti and Do, I've got a joke
to tell. Monsoon, the rock star who was granted NSA
citizenship for his music, as Marilyn Monsoon, met Maynard

James Koenan in the bathroom, in the bathroom, in the bathroom. That's it! Ha ha ha ha. Oh yes, and do they both have the eyes of Homer? Was Homer blind but can now he see?"

"I bring you! Ti and Do!" Suddenly on television, millions of people saw Ti and Do come out of doors at opposite ends of the high courts, and said "He has to live, he has to die, he has to live, he has to die. Do, you have to die. No, Ti, you have to die. We have to die, we have to die." But this happened last. And it was not their doubles or their fourthquels, triples or hexagles, it was their twentytoodles, the age of HATTILLA HATTILLA when he wrote *Ti has to die, No, Do has to die, No, they have to die.* At first came the persona of the theme of forced-suicide-murder, what Zeus did to Pandora, his wife and all the ancient Gods of Mycenae, when she came bearing a gift to society. In the future, HATTILLA HATTILLA lived in her home in Hahei, for Lymphis was in the Coromandel of New Zealand and was Mycenae, at the age of Atlantis, which was in Europe and on the Moon, and Atlantis flew with spaceships to the moon of Pluto and landed on it and all the Plutonians cut their heads and hands off with chainsaws. For if you land on a moon that is around a planet with intelligent life on it, they kill themselves. Anyway, HATTILLA HATTILLA lived in Hahei, and this house was where Pandora lived. She lived in an execution chamber and Zeus, her husband, had frequent visits to it to meet her, ending up chopping off her head with an axe. She attended Dilworth school in Lymphis, where James Blood lived, a cannibal, and whoever eats hearts and brains is an immortal, and had his castle above the Senior school but also beside, left and right; it was on pillars to the heavens. She used to say "Don't tell" in her room behind the pictures of Isabella and James Dilworth, a cage, seeing HATTILLA HATTILLA looking at the penis area of another student (though not bisexual he decided) and saying "Don't tell" so no one told and so no one knew, and this effected him since he saw her through time, since the time continuum merged because he was an albino. And he got a word stress disorder and felt pain at the phonemes in the words "Don't tell."

He saw her one day walk into his yard. And she said "Hi, I'm Pandora. I read Pandora's People when you were afflicted with your word stress disorder one time I said "Don't tell,"" for when she said "Don't tell" his consciousness split and he went into a coma and time unravelled and she could see him, "and I wrote HATTILLA's People. I'm in love with you."

At this stage HATTILLA HATTILLA was turning into a superhuman albino. He was seeing symbols of halcyon, esoteric and cosmological Song of Sillity of Might (which batman play we'll get to later) and hearing a voice of the ancients that lived in universe before universe that had similar traits of superhuman ability that they gained like him, through schizophrenia. They said, one speaking to each symbol, "Rose window sclera, black flame hair. A scanner adjustment system in the middle of your forehead" et cetera, and he changed, his head spinning around. But this was after the time travelling dimension, the Unverae dimension- which has a castle in a vast garden and coloured portals in the sky and in walkways to time travel, with a rainbow-smudged-sky, the castle being built there by the ancients, it used to being just a coloured, warped dimension to time travel, now colonised, with paintings in the castle of time immemorial- tuned him while he was watching a DVD and told him to move the numbers on the DVD player, and he did, with the LOADING word appearing while the DVD was still playing, and fragmented numbers flying across the DVD player. He was using telekinesis. He was a telekinetic. "That's great!" they said, sitting on computers in the dimensional point at the Unverae constellation, a civilisation point that was a set of buildings and houses where they lived, humans, immortal humans, though now becoming cannibals as Pandora's People spread to them and they read it and caught a mental virus. They ate the brains and hearts of their dead children, and were immortals.

This was after the dimensions opened up to him and he was invited to go to the dimensions. After they opened up, he heard an alien in an invisibility cloak walk across his lawn and a spaceship appeared in the sky of the Haratians, saying "We want Quantitative Machinisers!" Quantitative Machinisers were machines that used space-time orbital patterns to time travel into the past, and were used by the FBI to find who killed who at a murder scene and used by the CIA to find who killed JFK. If you look closely at the Zapruder tape, you'll see a Quantitative Machiniser behind JFK's head before he's shot.

The albino dimension opened up, where he could philosophise about albinohood. The Psychic dimension opened up, where he could philosophise the hardest philosophy of all, Psychic philosophy. And the Invera dimension, dimension of depression and philosophy itself and the Unverae, dimension of time travel.

They broadcasted on Fox news and told jokes, the civilisation points on the news as well, who controlled the dimensions, founded by civilisations long ago. But oh! They spoke, for the first time about the energy wane of the universe and how energy was waning and the universe would end but how it won't end anymore since there is a body in seven million, seven hundred and seventy seven thousand seven hundred and seventy seven dimensions. And it is the body of HATTILLA HATTILLA. They said if there is a body in this dimension the universe is immortal. The Aliens hated him, and said on the news, dancing, "Ba ba, ba ba, ba ba ba, ba ba ba, ba ba, ba ba ba!" taking the Mickey Mouse out of him. Mickey Mouse was a god that used to do double vision in front of mirrors and gained intelligence from this Eye Chasm Reading, which can lead you to develop psychosis and in HATTILLA HATTILLA's case, see the eye of cloning, a monobrow and an eye in the middle of the pyramid, which is the darkness of satan, God's spaceship. The darkness of Satan is God's spaceship. After that he created five universes.

So Pandora met him on that day, as he turned superhuman and Fox news had a satellite camera on him, and afterwards, the next day, he showed that just because his brain is a small sphere brain, doesn't mean he doesn't have intelligence. And he made it bigger and smaller. When he was younger he did double vision and his brain came out of his nose and he ate it and it appeared in his head again. It was a sphere brain as large as his head only made out of frontal lobes. He did this with his eyes as well and when he was in Hamilton hospital he made a video image on his iris of an albino him with spiky hair saying "You're walking through your shadow, aren't you, HAATTILLLLAAA!" and disappeared. When he was at home before he made the Tree of Life drink, since his heart stopped beating he electrified himself to get it beating again but it didn't work, and then he went ot the mirror and did the same he did in Hamilton hospital, walked through his shadow three times moving his vision down and up in his third eye as he was going crosseyed and he saw Michael Mathew, death himself, come to him as he electrified himself but he split his word stress disorder and HATTILLA said "Drink me death!;" so death drunk him from a silver cup, and he teleported from him. Death could not kill him now, since he bet him once. However Death, Michael Mathew, and there are many Michael Mathews, cheated and came to him in his dreams. He dreamed of the top financer saying he died of brain cancer and his body was the body of Marilyn Monsoon, the rock star granted NSA citizenship, with the name Monsoon, and the top financer was saying "He died of brain cancer, brain cancer, brain cancer!" and then he saw death's pattern in the wall and it said 9.5 B + and he solved it in his mind, and it was A-, the mark he scored for his English paper at Auckland university.

At Auckland University in his Ancient Greek History class he made the Lecturer go insane as he put words in his head and he said "Cuckoo!" The lecturer went insane because he kept on doing space time continuum conversions, converging the future or past with the present by moving his hands, saying "He has to die," while pointing down and up. The Art teacher of Dilworth film college did this and her future self time travelled back to her present in assembly and her present self killed her future self and her future self said before "Don't kill me, don't kill me!" The head of Dilworth did this many times and there were seven of him. But they all started killing each other, and there was left with none at the end, all disappearing; the last two battling over Keda and dying both together.

"I am the soul of force-suicide-murder, and I will scare you shitless! I will terr-ror-fy you!" and moved his hands up and down, "But I'm his double!" and another one came in, all covered in scars and razor marks, marks of suicide, for forced suicide murder is when someone pressurs someone to kill themselves, which is the worst crime imaginable. And then Pandora came in through the door, "I am Pandora, and I will terrify you." She lipped, for she had no tongue for it was chopped off by Zeus when he cut off her head with an axe. But she was Nearly-Headless-Pandora.

When HATTILLA HATTILLA saw her head get chopped off in a space time conversion, for she did one when he was there outside the toilet (she was killed in the toilet), he saw her head get chopped off. Saddened, he went outside and saw her coffin. He then was victim of a space time continuum conversion that Pandora did nearly dead, and HATTILLA HATTILLA with a beating of his brain-heart, brought her back to life. But, it was not enough and she died. However, before she died, she carved the name HATTILLA into the Pinnacles in the Coromandel and put a library in there of literature of her own, including her greatest work, HATTILLA's People. The Pinnacles in the Coromandel is the entrance to Shambala, the mystical Tibetan city for the Tibetans mated with the Maoris on Stewart Island before the Europeans came to New Zealand.

Then Ti and Do came in, not their doubles or triples, the real Ti and Do, but there are two sets of Ti and Dos, but the Ti and Dos that were victims of forced suicide murder, as well as Pandora, were there, and they spoke "He has to live, he has to die. Do has to die. No, Ti has to die. No, they have to die!"

Pandora's People said, his arms spinning as he summoned, "Come to Hahei or Miami beach to see Pandora's People live! Witness the characters and see it like you've never seen it before! You will see HATTILLA HATTILLA take his life on the Pa and televised on Miami beach, and you'll see his soul kill himself repeatedly, summoning his soul many times!"

With this he left, then crashed his car into the gymnasium again and was cloned.

6. I am Villie

Two Haratians stood. They stared. Their open eyes, grey, were on the sight of silver thunderbolts from a black moon over a planet with a golden thunderstorm. They shared emotions and shuddered. They were tall and lean, aliens, with long oval heads and long, slender bodies that were grey and yellow. One spoke, "Black thunderbolts from the pupil, over a gold centred and blue iris, and black moon pupils, the right eye of a planetary system" They continued standing. Around them more planets were seen, one green, one yellow and one blue, another ocean planet; stars were seen in the distance. Behind the eye were two orange suns, aqua leaking from them in folds and lighting up the planets. They hovered. From the living room a silver being walked left towards them, slowly walking towards them, he was solid, silver and safe, a Muhumagian; he came from the distant consellation of Sonar the Silver and his name was Michael Mathew. Their was one of his kind in the spaceship crew of nine, two Haratians, an Abducbcioaiian, an Abducian, a Plebian, a Sorvanian, a Sorkonian a Human and a Gevian. The Gevian was sitting down, slowly drinking wine. In dark, deep and azure space VILLIE, Yellow and grey, hovered in darkness, shrined in the light of stars and concreted in constellations. It sat still, while the crew looked at the planetary constellation. It was shaped like an oval with a straight line at the end and a sharper point at the front. With an open circle at the end, that was grey, with a circle opening for the booster; and grey and yellow wings, two wings, on either side.

A green hand moved, with a green aura moving about it, as she made hand gestures, while the Sorvanian, named Sophie Silver spoke, "It's time to move to the Gravian constellation to land on Prebata, I'm not sure if Prebata is there or not, goddess that she is, but we need to find her. This eye is surely a key, as Question said, what did he say again... "...to find the key, is to look into goldeneye..." We have stared into the goldeneye, Mathena and Sarah moer than others and we have found something. There is something about the sea accepting the black htunderbolts, and though its empty, it drinks the cup full. That means, we have found something, Prebata went here along time ago, and she is tied to this place, she lost something here, her ideal, to become a plawright. She spent her time talking and singing, an opera singer, but it is here that Sylvia Nonia spoke those fatefull words, "To become a playwriitght is to become a pirate, sailing the seven seas, the seven words that complete a play, for a play is always completed, though a poem is always unfinished, and to become a pirate, a playwright is to become a wanderer, do you want to be a wanderer Prebabta? A composer always searching for the seventh key? Or a singer always singing the seventh key, guarded, safe and secure, at peace, with allowance; not searching forever...what shall your fateful hand beknight?" Those were the words Syliva spoke to her at this planetary constellation, Tyllen, a long time ago, before the great years of her singing Fiuralls carmens. It's time to leave, what we have gained here is insight. We have tread the water and scanned it, and we have found a dress of hers. It is soft satin, a red dress, slim and revealing. It was one of her favourite dresses. It's time to leave." Sarah agreed, an Abducbcioaiian and the captain. She was short and had a body made out of wilotif, a harder compound than diamond, and was the colour of wood chips, a body with two hands and two legs, like the rest of them. She had a flat head at the top, with a curved chin and large, open, circular eyes and her body looked like itwas encrusted with jewels. She spoke, "It's time to leave, no more flesh and bone here of Prebata, its time to pass the test, time to leave. Our next destination is the planet named Prebata." With that they left the planet Fillonian and the Tevenian consteallation with a space time continuum planeshift, that moved the spaceship into dark space and then they put on their boosters. They moved incandesccently.

A small planet came into view and they landed in a desert.

The scent of roses was in the air. White, snowy mountains perched beneath Lofloriens; below, in the village, rainbows sang Sillity, rose, and falling between the knitted houses from the coloured gardens and, standing before them, the yellow sign said "Prebata". Red letters, bent from the rivers currents said "Prebatom", "Prebatum and "Prebatem." Michael said, "Four names for a village, the currents seem to show that they always shape the name that way." Lofloriens shone reflected in the river, a blue, a yellow and a red. A blue path winded from the village through the desert. Light cast from the houses lit it up. Three coloured lights made an abduction silloueght and aural mirages in the desert while yellow lines of light streamed from their bodies. The scent of roses was in the air from the village before them. The village stood around 100 metres away, but they quietly stood, gaping, having found a village. Sophie gingerly placed her foot forward and the others followed. They moved forward slowly, their shoes slowly moving forward through the dust in the desert and they came to the front of the path. The path sides were covered in sand, and they slowly moved onto it, Sophie second; Mathena first; Mandrake third; Michael fourth and Sarah fifth. They slowly trailed the track, their shadows cojoining. There were lamp shades on the sides of the path and they could see clearly. They walked and walked, and slowly they came to the edge of the village. There was a opening there and they walked through it, out onto the footpath by the street. They kept walking for some time until what appeared to be amarried couple came over to them. They introduced themselves as Reeana and Gerald. They spoke fluent English. Once having told them that their spaceship had only just landed for repairs, they said they would take them to a house t ostay for the night, or however long they wanted to stay.

Reeana and Gerald escorted them around, and around the roads, untill they came to a medium sized house, white with a blue roof, street lights out front, that had no tenants. "Here it is," said Gerald. And walked them towards it. The wooden white door was opened and they were taken inside, the lights turned on. It wasn't a mystery how they got their electricity, their was a small power station on one of the main roads they passed. Fully furnished, the house was in a fine condition. They placed their bags down near the kitchen, on the living room floor. The villager, Reeana asked them for a drink of tea, they accepted, though they had drunk water not long before, and she sat them down on the duvon, on a slender cushioned wooden chair and on another couch. They prepared the tea and then stood to drink it out in the garden. They stood to drink it, while they sat down on the outside chairs. Reeana paused from her cup of tea, and looking with one eye to the stars and one eye to Sarah she spoke, "So where are you from? We know you came here in a spaceship, from the looks of things you crashed. I'm sure you'll be able to get things going again. We have a few engineers here. You're welcome in the village. We'll have a town meeting tomorrow, be sure to introduce yourselves. Time doesn't exist here, we never age. We've been married for 3000 years. Some of us have been around for millions. You're sure to find comfort here in the village. We're the only village left on the planet. There were other villages, but they've long since had people living in them. The last one was Stilum and they left 50,000 years ago. They unbuild their villages before they leave. Most probably you saw the village before you landed. We're surrounded by Lofloriens here. They have intelligence, and sometimes, very rarely, they go to war, great rods of plasma shoot out of them, and they appear as coloured beings, with red, blue or whatever colour of energy lines. At one time one came to the village inspecting the Unverae dimensional traveller Raspurgin. He's a time traveller, most probably you have heard of him before. Well he is from this planet, the name is Prebata, as you should have in your catalogue on your spaceship. Anyway, when Raspurgin was only 16 he built his first time machine and a Loflorien came to see it. He just looked at it then went away. Without touching it or anything. Strange things, those Lofloriens, most often they dissappear for years, then return and they can take on human form. We don't know why but these ones have been here for a long time without moving on. Others have disappeared for lengths of time. There's something very strange about them. Anyway, this is the only village left on our planet."

They were beautiful, she was in her 30s most probably and he in his 30s too but they seemed immortally old, for time had no workings here as they had heard.

She leaned towards Michael, her eyes large and brown, like full moons, surrounded by a haze of golden skin. "It's because of the forest that we don't age, it has mystical workings, it's its trees, the scent of them, what kind they are. The creatures in the forest have lived there for immortal years."

Red ridges swept across the cliff face. As Sophie Silver stood, her arms at her side, aqua bolts of lightning at the seas horizon struck, jagged and scattered and the thunder rolled above, ahead and all around. Below, waves, green, crashed and the sea spray washed over Sophie Silver, gently wetting her breasts, as they shone and shone in the milky twilight. Of the flat she stood, her left eye framed around her cheek bone and forehead, green, staring at the horizon, ever so slowly watching the lightning storms. She had just been into the forest with Raspurgin, travelling through the Unverae dimension, and she reflected on sleeping with Raspurgin in the castle. The forest haunted her.

Now she knew the truth about her spaceship, which it was built for, why it was built and more, what it is capable of doing. She reflected on her engineering work on the spaceship, and all the cords she thought what they knew they did. How it had the power to do space time continuum plane shifts, and how the other spaceships are returning to claim it. It was built by some of the villagers 5 million years ago, in a forest village with the same name as this one, which was shifted outside of the forest after it was sold for gold to build a better spaceship, and inverted and obverted octagon, so it can space time jump, being inverted and space time warp, being obverted. It had a golden energy transversion shield. If only they knew where her spaceship was. But did they really want it? What did they really want with the spaceship?

Lightning was still striking. Two lines of soft footsteps to the left of her were heard, and Sarah and Michele walked over to her. Sophie wept, and they held her in their arms, "I slept with Raspurgin in the Unverae dimensional castle. He was so gentle and so sweet. But I've found out the truth about the village and what they want with our spaceship. They want it for space time continuum plane shifts, to shift the village and for trade, but more importantly, they want it to be entirely disconnected from the forest, that forest Villie. The forest is connected to the village still. They need the spaceship to be united with the older villagers, so the forest doesn't control them anymore. With the spaceship, time continuous, they'll age. To not age is a blessing, but to not age because of the forest is something else entirely. And the forest still holds contentment to them; they need contentment from somewhere else. And they're building another spaceship, as you've heard, an inverted and obverted octagon, that cannot time travel, though moves at the speed of light."

Sarah and Michele held Sophie in their arms. "It's OK Sophie, we may return for Raspurgin again, but right now we have a more important mission, as a spaceship crew to return again to our home civilisation. Sarah is in love with Minolto, and I'm sure we'll return for him as well. He's a beautiful man, so is Raspurgin. But are they really for life? You both don't have husbands at home, though I'm sure you'll meet somebody else. But I'm glad there is an old repairs workshop in the forest. We can do a space continuum plane shift there, since the main hub is still working, all we need to do is fix the main thrive. As the medic I'm happy we're leaving, though I haven't fallen in love. Though I went and saw Ti and Do, those magicians, and they're absolutely terrifying, that was after I saw Song of Sillity of Might, the play, no, they came on before the play started. Their performance was a skit. It was about this civilisation called Nonia, and in Nonia, cloning is started. They start to clone through a black obelisk. It's called the red potato. And then there's the TV King, who advertises it, then there's a goddess called Sylvia, who killed herself, though rather nearly did, though actually faked her death, and she's cloned. Anyway her clones end up marketing the obelisk to the masses and everyone comes to be cloned, for she was such a star. She has a homunculus called Homunculus Cray, he follows her around. Anyway, there's a character called Sylvia's People who markets it as well, who is unclonable, then he has all these doubles, then there's another one, called Sylvia's People as well, who's not his double, or his triple, who's been cloned a number of times and who is the head of the cloning division. Anyway there's a boy called Hattilla Hattilla who becomes an albino. He becomes an albino with human superpowers. He gets 11 ribs, 11 spinal cords, a brain heart, another heart, 3 folded bones, primary energy and matter chakras and astral and tectonic abilities. He leads a revolt against the cloning and ends up winning with the help of a private investigator, who investigates a character called the godfather, who is the head of a major business corporation. Anyway, it only went on for about 5 minutes, but that play, Song Of Sillity Of Might, it was fantastic and hauntingly beautiful.

We stepped into the time machine, the purple light folding our bodies. It's so beautiful in there, with the purple light, a large rectangle in the middle. It has everything he needs, a bed, a controlling centre, everything. I watched him as we flew above the planet while he was in the controlling centre and then he configured it to the Unverae dimension. He moved the controls forward and typed into the keypad and we were off. Space bent and multitudes of colours blurred and became fine blotches and blurs of colour. We were in the Unverae dimension. The first thing I noticed was the castle. It was huge and grey, in the middle of a garden that was so green and beautiful, neatly cut hedges are all within it. And the roses...the roses. There were many roses; red roses, blue roses, yellow roses, the stuff of rose blood; the scent of them, beautiful, when we were out of the time machine. We landed in the garden; the castle was behind a gently sloping hill. It was an old grey castle, with one tall tower. We went into the castle, and there were paintings everywhere, like the time travellers path. He checked the records book to see if we could go into the forest and we left, walking back down the path onto the time traveller's path; there were paintings everywhere, old as time memorial. Blurs of colours were everywhere behind the arches off the path. He decided on one and we walked through the arch, then he moved some numbers with his hand on the blurs of colours and we walked through a portal, into a distant field above a forest. The forest was sprawling."

Suddenly a cheek, golden, shone in the darkness, was softly lit by the lamp and his mouth was red. He opened it and spoke, "My name is Minolto Winolto, and your name must Sarah, commander Sarah." Slowly turning the lamp with his hand extended, the branches and trees were lit up, branches close by, leaves hazy in the mist. Tall and lean, he was also extraordinarily handsome, his face a soft tan, his lips red, his face oval and spherical in proportions and with blue eyes, brown hair to his medium sized ears, hanging like fruit, ready to be plucked in a sexual escapade. Sarah had heard his name before and seen his works, the painter, greater than Hoffman, Karaon and Fenal. She remembered their works, remembering walking, her footsteps echoing in a gallery, seeing a great work, the work of Karaon, "Beautiful Wanderings," the soft blue of the solitary between two planets, standing in a spaceship, beautiful full red and white planets, with orbital moon shadow from two moons, one lime white, the other aqua blue and yellow, softly painted, with blotches of a soft fire of colour around the edges. The wanderer had no name, but was simply known as "the Blue," He was only but profoundly a wash of blue paint with eyes reflecting moons and the colours of the planets. She had seen Minoltos work before. His hands were not creased; they were as smooth as plums and were tanned and golden. He was a great painter. He started leading the way back to the village, though seemed to take a different turn, "There's something I want to show you before we go back. It's the entrance to the forest. Maybe we could go in their sometime. But we won't go there. It's not dangerous at all on this planet but it's too late tonight.

The Loflorien was uncoloured, simply a light blue clear colour, the colour of water; she flew in, then, arching his back upwards, landed; he slowly became coloured looking, shape shifting into a normal, beautiful human. She spoke, "My name is Cynthia, I know that you're searching for Prebata and I've heard word of her. A man named Raspurgin, a time traveller, found her eye shadow, called ROSEBLOOD in the Unverae castle, in front of the main bedroom mirror; he's kept it. He's from this planet, and at the moment he is travelling from the Unverae constellation group. The star constellation that safeguards the Unverae dimensional point. Surely you've heard his name before. He'll return in two days time, if you could wait until then you'll hear what he has to say and the ROSEBLOOD may lead a clue to her current whereabouts. She was there not that long before Raspurgin found it. She must have been there with the Avucians, if she was abducted,

"My name is Raspurgin." Held atop the only route to the forest was the melting sun, softly setting on the icy, smooth mountain top. That was my first thought and sight, as I stepped through the gateway from the Unveraod dimension. How many times I had spoken that line, and then always confronted with mystery from mystery balls. Planets hovered above the grand, vast and full garden of the Unveraod, next to the castle and the other garden of the Unverae dimension. Planets full of life of times ancient in the past from myriad universes. Each coloured like candy, slowly spinning measured around 50 times my height in the dimensions proportions. I came again from the time traveller dimension, known as the Unveraod, right next to the Unverae dimension.

7. The Rose Blood of Pandora

Great Lucifer rose, his rose on his forehead slowly spinning as he was confronted with Pandora. His heart was the heart of Pandora, as he lost his heart as he fell down from the Primavera universe a long time ago, and was reborn as Lucifer again in this final universe of the white space universes. Pandora said, "We need the crown of schizophrenia to create a dark space universe. We seek the sights of psychosis, and its hold on the pure obsession of sights and sounds. They seek Rose Blood, others seek God, but we seek psychosis. Do you know where to find it?" and she laughed magnificently, "No, of course you don't. But you nearly found it in your great sleep didn't you? Tormented with my visage as I cast you into hell! Hell and heaven are both death, and there is no separating the two." She came in closer through the great opening of the black hole castle, as Lucifer walked to the left, terrified of God but keeping up a visage of stability, and her white, orange, red and yellow hair was flaming, casting shadows of gold and silver on the dark and vivid black walls of the dark hole castle. "I can nearly breathe psychosis. Did you know, once attaining psychosis, you can change your body; it creates the ultimate art forms! Our flaming hair, the rose window sclera of the Arians, the eye chasms of the Minolto Winolto's, all comes from a branch of schizophrenia, or if put another way, psychosis. We experience depression, happiness and all emotion in its heights but we still have not reached it. But, alas! I have found where it is hidden. It is hidden in our brains, and to bring it out, you need to taste Rose Blood, Lotus Blood, Dandelion Blood or the Blood of Blossoms! I know where to find Rose Blood, and I am yet to create it, in the past, in the rose universe. It is the rose universe itself. You just need to unfold a rose in the Inveraod dimension, and then you see the tombs of Satan and God! Our tombs! I see my death and the death of Satan, you, in my greatest moments for I have done it, and I have Rose Blood and the three spaceships are after me more, for they not only seek to kill God but they also seek to attain Rose Blood. The Inveraod dimension is full of humans and aliens now that want to attain Rose Blood, but they lack the IQV average and water blood, strength of mind and agility to attain it!

"Rose Blood is mysterious. None knew what it was. It's the blood of roses in your veins, and once attaining it, you experience psychosis, it's a drug produced by the brain once you have unfolded a rose in the Inveraod dimension. I experienced psychosis and I have come to you in my previous form. I shape shifted to not surprise you, for I know that your heart is weak and is not your own, but mine, and I have come to you third to show you my new form and my power to create a dark space universe. It's a holy drug, and one not to be tried lightly as it gives one schizophrenia. God is now a schizophrenic and the first psychotic, and I shall create a dark space universe for my form has accelerated beyond all evolution. I am now a zeleenzetrialeen and a zalbino, and a zampire and a zarian and a Rose Bloodian. I will show you my form."

Saying this, she slowly moved her white hand upwards and drew a rose on her forehead, the pattern you draw on your forehead to shape shift, and shape shifted. Roses curled around her form, in colours of dark space, vivid in the white walls of the castle in the white hole.

Lucifer saw her then, her red hair rose petals and moving like shooting stars, and thunderbolts of blue Pandorie colour for her legs, and galaxies and universes along like tattoos up her arms. And a long dress that was Yin and yang, the dress that TI wears, strangely, and her eyes were black holes, not white but black. She moved her hands upward, and centred them, then created dark space in a small circle within her hands, and said "Behold dark space. What the new universes shall be. They shall be made of dark space. No more of the white space universes shall come, only the black ones, the dark ones, the ones that speak no doom. And after the Big Boom they shall come with a Big Bang!"

Speaking this she left the castle, walking out into her spaceship, a blue rose, the Rose spaceship of Pandora, which

Villie, The Grey and the Wackiness were all constantly searching for; and the Rose spaceship that the angels Ti and Do were seeking. Rose Blood was not the cloning rose, but a drug, and the so called Rose Bloodians of Ti and Do that were cloned were hoaxes, though they had power, and were not the race of the Rose Blood.

.

8. Dita Von Teese Dances in a Cut Wrist

A wrist, red and cut, rose from the ground beside the White
House of Death and the White Tree, it was large, taller than
two bodies, and Pandora stood in the slit singing, "Ti and Do,
they have to die! I have to die, you have to live! She has to
die, he has to live!" and "I soon shall drown in this wrist of
blood and death!"

The stars were white and pointed, once moved into
positions of humans holding their arms up, inspiring and
noble, but tonight they looked as if they were moving above
Pandora; becoming larger and spiralling down towards her.
Soon they came into view and Pandora's swan song was
caught on flying cameras all around her, probing into her
space and time; they were black and had wires spouting out of
them, and looked like flying insects with syringes. They held
her in their view and she was soon on TV all around Nonia in
her cut wrist singing.

Pandora, wearing a white dress, brought up a razor and cut
her bottom lip off, and millions of fans of hers around Nonia
of the singer, actress and celebrity saw her do it and copied
her in mock act.

She started singing:

"I lived, for what seem like a million years
In Nonia and the time has come to kill
Myself! I no longer want to live! I've
Come to grow a cut wrist out of the ground
With witch magick; the old pentacle star
I am, an inverted star soon to be a
Black hole! Little rose, little rose, little rose dead!"

Having sung, she took another lip off with her razor and
cut off her entire face and tongue, dropping it into the gaping
red hole in the wrist and started dancing; a white and red
balloon as her face, swinging her hips to and throw. She then
stopped and slid down the wrist like in a children's
playground in Nonia, and started walking to Death Valley.
She took a look at the White Tree and saw photos of herself
having grown there, images of her as a star from the age of

youth to just before her present and new images of her without her face. She still had her eyes, for she didn't want to part with them yet.

She walked through the marshes until she came to Death Valley to what appeared to be a Hollywood Walpurgis Night. Fans of hers were around a tall pyramid made out of cut off parts of their faces and it appeared to be slowly turning inside and out and condensing. She stood there watching and it soon made itself into a homunculus made out of pieces of cut of people's faces. It was in the shape of a love heart and was grey, and said, "Evening Pandora, I am Homunculus Cray. I'll be your guide." She saw standing on a mountain of TV's the rock star Monsoon, who was granted NSA citizenship and was singing about Televisions and the soon to come TV King. Pandora didn't know who the TV King was, and stepped away to another sight. Soon bruised faces were spinning around her, and old actors from films past were appearing and dancing to the music of old radios.

Pandora left the Hollywood Walpurgis Night and walked to End Park, where the river ends and the Black Clown kills his children at the Shopgun Doors. She came to End Park and walked into a white river. There she came out white and looked like a sperm. She walked back to the love heart of her fans and it walked with her to the Shopgun Doors. There a picture of a child was above a shop with a huge shotgun coming out as the door and the Clown was standing on a motorbike with many of his children in front of him. He said, "Welcome to the shopgun doors, my dear. Whoever enters shall see Native Americans and the TV source, a grey portal to the collective unconscious."

Pandora heard him and entered through the mouth of the shotgun with Homunculus Cray. Beyond the walk-through she saw Native Americans at machinery seemingly holding society together and a grey eye of TV grey, and walked hesitantly, a white being, and drowned in the grey pit. There she came out into a court room with rainbows on the walls.

"You're cloned!" a judge said. And then she split into three bodies. One appeared in outer space and fell down onto a beach with sunbathers and drowned in the sea. The other died of a heart attack and Pandora was left, the original, and entered a bomb coffin with pink paint and an oxygen mask. She put the oxygen mask on and her funeral began.

Thence she was pushed on four wheels along a road with millions of fans on the side of the street holding photos of her that slowly dissolved in acid rain that began and they dissolved to. She came to the end of the road and was in the Non Lands where the candy coloured people lived. Here she lived until the time of Hattilla Hattilla.

A machine, grey, hauntingly beautiful, a cyborg with machine skin, stood on television next to a black monolith and said "Come to Nonia, to be beautiful and intelligent. You'll be turned into a superhuman through this black monolith. You'll be everything you desire."

Ti and Do said, "He has to die, no, she has to die!" when the TV was still on, and still people flocked to Nonia to be cloned. They walked in to the advertising of a machine Pandora and the talking on microphone of the TV King, who was talking about being cloned and advertised it on international TV.

Ti and Do said when the people were gathered, "She is the black obelisk, the machine Pandora; the black monolith. Stupidity is more eternal than love. He has to die, she has to die; no, they have to die!"

Soon everyone in the world was cloned and Venus was driving down the road on her carriage where no cameras were for everyone wanted cameras to be on them, and said to a suitor, "Come to the ball room party, I'll be there."

People flocked to this ball room party and there razors swung cutting off the limbs of the partiers and all was left was blood and death. Soon everyone in Nonia and around the world was dead from violence and end times, Armageddon.

But in the holes underneath the earth there were the rebels and those who chose not to be cloned and who watched the world hang like Jesus on his cross.

They came out of their Agatha's and took the world back. But it had changed, for Hattilla Hattilla transformed into an albino and Ti and Do rose again.

Hattilla Hattilla has to live, for he just turned into an albino. He saw a white rose in his mind, a developing psychosis and a voice that said "Albino skin" and just now he heard a voice that said rose window sclera and a scanner adjustment system on his forehead to scan universes, a roseum thornycum energy transversion shield, where if someone tries to kill him, they'd pick a rose from his force field; a seven seven inverted body to space time jump, where if someone tries to kill him again, he'd jump around the knife or warp. And it said black flame hair.

He was beautiful; he was an Aryan, an Arian, and an Eleenzetrialeen with eleven fingers on each hand and albino skin.

It was the 18nth of October and his birthday, and Ti and Do found out he was turning into an albino.

In the personal quarters of Ti and Do black, flittering and evanescent shadows around a mirror danced as Ti and Do applied their makeup for tonight's performance at Hattilla Hatttilla's birthday party. They were whispering to each other, brother and sister, "No, he has to die," "No, she has to die," "No, Ti has to die," "No, Do has to die" and together, "No, they...have...to...die!" Made up, before the mirror, their hair was fizzy; one black, the other white. Avuncular eye shadow crept up on each, around each others eyes, slowly curving upwards and downwards beyond the edges, purple and pretty, with gold lines bordering it. Yin and Yang was the dress Do wore, balanced with black and white shadow and light and the suit Ti wore was an Astral Eye, with aqua blue eyes spotted all along it. Dressed to kill, they finished applying their white and black make up. White make up for Do, black for Ti. The holy stamp of Rose Blood was on their foreheads, a image of a rose painted out of blood; ancient and ghastly. Ti and Do, The Insider and The Outsider were obsessed with Roses and mystery. They chattered and sang in their apartment as they prepared for tonight's performance.

They arrived at Hattilla Hattilla's birthday party and performed but he wasn't there. He was in outer space, his body as a spaceship since that was one of the powers that he received.

A hooded man in the high courts was sitting an IQ test and scored 124, then drank a glass of milk with chocolate in it and said "I passed." Then said, "I just had a heart attack!"

It was Pandora's People, the character in Hattilla Hattilla's play, like Ti and Do, but it was written in the 5th dimension and when you write a play in the fifth dimension the characters come to life and inhabit the real world. So the world had been taken over by Ti and Do from Hattilla Hattilla's play before with the black obelisk and now it was taken over again with a new character finishing off the cloning called the Godfather. But he was put out of business by the old rebels and no one was cloned, but Pandora's People was now summoning doubles of Ti and Do in the high courts and the souls of "forced suicide murder" that was done to the real Ti and Do, who killed themselves after having suffered forced suicide murder, when someone tries to make you kill yourself which is an act of murder. They appeared covered in bruises and scars, and soon Hattilla Hattilla was on the streets in a white hood chanting, "No he has to die, no she has to die" with Pandora's People, the name of his play, now a character himself in a black hood, and he was saying the same thing. People were terrified, and flocked back to their houses but Ti and Do were growing out of their yards.

9. Arab-Ham Linking

Tears of winter broke from the canopy of the stars, and the hellish Pa stood firm yet broken, an icon of the horror, and the waters of Hahei beach were quiet, still; yet collecting the rain, and the sky was like an open eyelid of a shy suicide. A white river was the sand, an albino arm with phosphorescent stars and the village was asleep with wine. But the Suicides of Stars of States were awaking in Hahei!

A purple bruise, a top hat, a black hood with an albino forehead, a dent in the head of Do, all arose from the waters of Hahei this night, and Ti arose his frame covered in bruises and marks of murder and forced suicide murder, an afro of black and black eyeliner, smeared from the water, and the white afro of Do, with eyeliner also smeared, gold coloured for both, and Pandora's People awoke in his black hood, that pallid albino personification of the play Pandora's People written by Michael Mathew. O! The Characters of Suicide Star State and Pandora's People had come to life! And Abraham Lincoln arose from the waters of this collective unconscious, in a black suit and top hat, and Suicide Star State himself arose, and Pandora, O, Pandora, my dear, dear Pandora-

Pandora rose from blue space, a beauty queen, with fame eyes, fame lips, fame eyeliner, and a catwalk smile and catwalk teeth and a catwalk hairline. She had blonde hair and orange petal teeth and was the first to rise from the waters, and she shivered from the cold of the rain on the albino arm, in a dress drenched by the sea; a Yin and Yang dress, black and white. Her warm eyes took in the Pa, and she screamed, saying "Why have you forsaken me?"

Ti and Do were dancing on the beach, saying "We're alive but we have to die, Do, you have to die. No, Ti, you have to die. No, we have to die. We're alive but we have to die. God and Satan are dead but they have to die, God has to die. No, Satan has to die. No, they have to die. No, Michael Mathew who wrote us back to life has to die! He has to, he has to die!

He has two hearts, he has to die!"

Then Pandora's People took in the site of the Pa and said, "Why have you forsaken me?"

Abraham Lincoln took in the site of the Pa and uttered, "Why have you forsaken me, O Lord?"

Suicide Star State took in the site of the Pa and spoke, "Why have you forsaken me, my Michael Mathew?"

And the Pa spoke to them, the voices of dying children, "We're alive but we're heading to death, maybe we'll get to see you soon. Maybe we'll get to see you soon!"

10. You'll be an Albino Soon

Antony Underwest hung in dark space, about to shiver, about to shine, about to see himself in third person walking in the doorway from where he will be in bed. He shivers, he is shiny, sweaty, he is hearing voices, the voice saying "You had a word stress disorder. You used to feel pain at the words 'Don't tell' and you have just had it unbedded. You were raped and molested when they used to split your consciousness at saying the words and it will all come back to you. Remember, on the eighteenth of October you had a nervous breakdown. Thank you, for this beautiful experience"

Scared, he walks through the musty corridors of Saint Josephs and sees it as the heart of his school, Blood school for boys from straightened circumstances, where James Blood, the founder, lived, and sold his urine in wine bottles for people on the street. But he sees this short man also living above, around and beside the school, a code, meaning he lived above the senior school on pillars which was his farm, in a castle, and also under the school, in a bone church, made out of the bones of Maoris who died in the New Zealand wars. And Antony sees his grave, at the junior school, but sees his body in the senior school hall, where black robed people are doing an ancient ritual right this minute, saying "Come, come, come" and evoking his spirit, trying to turn him into James Blood. He sees that he had experienced this before, when he was a high school student, and he turned into James Dilworth and walked around the grass with the head of the trust board, and said "Why aren't these children being eaten?" Antony sees cannibals, and a man named Raspurgin who he escaped with him from under the senior school where his old seventh formers were having a feast of human mean and were about to eat him himself. But his old seventh formers he sees as doubles of the real students, with the real school beneath the school, and they are vicious cannibals with sharp teeth and a Mormon who wants to eat the golden eyed one, which will be him, Antony Underwest thinks.

He sees an organ spaceship under the Blood trust board,

made out of brains and hearts and sees the principle, Michael Mathew, shoot a bolt of electricity through it and it flew, hovering, to the ceiling. He sees cloning machines under the trust board and boys with half of their brains eaten with spoons in their heads. He sees maximum pain and maximum heart attack machines and hears a voice "We will put you in maximum pain and maximum heart attack for absolute years for you're turning into an Arian, and an Aryan, and an Albino. We want to eat your brain for your IQ points, and then the principle will become an Arian, a flame haired albino with a long body that can fly through space and stretch into black holes."

"A Japanese man is coming to stab you in the heart, and you will choke on diet coke" the voice says and he drifts into the manager's room where he asks to lie in bed, and sleep for the night for he is not feeling well. "Sure," he says, and sexually utters, "You know, I'm always here for you when you need it."

He doesn't sleep; he falls softly into the endless void of psychosis, and waits staring at the clock seeing himself being molested by all the people that split his word stress disorder. He sees a spaceship buried one hundred feet under Dilworth school and sees that they need his heart, cut out, to open up the lock around the spaceship, but it is with his second heart, for he is an Eleenzetrialeen. Someone born with two hearts in their chest, and hearts in their fingertips and toes and a heart for a brain, a brain heart, and he sees it, in eclipse with the sun; it is a sphere brain, made solely out of frontal lobes and soon he will have to control his own body. But, he will have two black hearts soon, and they will have body memory where they will beat on their own, once he has beat them a number of times.

11. The Cannibals Are Under the Earth

"The aliens are here," spoke John John, the private investigator JD had found, or Hattilla Hattila, or Antony Underwest. "The aliens are visiting, the aliens are abducting."

"We'll see them coming and we'll keep them inside," spoke Pandora's People, the personification of Michael Mathew's play, Jarrad Dickson's play, as he had turned into Michael Mathew, an aberration God of albinohood, with golden eyes and rose window sclera. "Why don't you go up there in your body, you know, your body is a spaceship, and zoom around like one of them Mathew?" spoke Pandora's People again. He was sweating. He was eating some chocolate and reading the NSE conspiracy theory manual. Michael Mathew read it in Hamilton hospital's mental health ward, the Henry Bennet Centre, in his dorm, looking up at the air conditioning plate and going cross eyed, scanning, and listened to the black building behind the NSA building that is the building of the NSE reading it.

They were in a Lamborghini Murcialago on the streets, with people on the streets, seeing eyes still in the sky and Ti and Do on the streets, saying "He has to live, he has to die." They were only doubles of Ti and Do, the real two sets of Ti and Do were evanescent, disappearing, in hiding. The ghosts from the moon of dead children were still visiting earth and terrifying everyone, and Michael Mathew's double was also on the streets in a Versace hood and robe, saying "He has to live, he has to die."

On there TV in the car the movie Song of Sillity of Might was playing, written first as twenty plays in HBC at Hamilton, and made into movies by Quentin Tarantino who also made Ti and Do and the Holy Products of Pandora as a movie, which was at the top of imbd.com's 250 greatest movies, writing by Jarrad Dickson, the aberration god.

"Are you still going to write "The HHH and the UEU and the OEO? Hattilla?" asked John John, "Or are you going to found them as secret services? The FBT, Forum Bureau of Technology? "

"Yeah, and I'm asking Monsoon to be the head of them," answered Jarrad Dickson, the albino Goddess, hermaphrodite God.

12. Song of Sillity of Might

Sillity awoke from her slumber, around purple roses she was sleeping. She softly and slowly sat up, raising her knees and smelling the perfume of the rich roses. She was not tired. Her flame hair billowed upwards, far upwards, towards a distant star that hung as the gravitational field that held the orbit of the planet Neptune. She was wide awake. Her eyes darted left and right, her red rose window irises slowly spinning as she slowly came back to consciousness. Suddenly a ghost appeared, the ghost of the Holy Ghost. It was short, with three bodies, silver and machine like, looking similar to Muhumagian women. It was conjoined between the shoulder blades by silver chords. It came down from high above, making no motion but its six eyes, ghostly empty, on her; and it made a motion with its hands, the motion of the Holy Chalice. Suddenly her breasts changed form, and jewels encrusted her breast bone abover her cleavage, wrapped in robes of coloured skin, flaming gold, yellow and orange blossoms. She was now the Holy Chalice. It spoke, "You are now the Holy Ghost." With that, it flew back upwards into the sky, not touching any of the purple roses in the field and disappeared into the black sky. She was suddenly slowly turning silver and her irises hovered before her eyeballs, rose window wheels that slowly spun in perfect circles around her face. She was the Holy Ghost. She stood up and pulled a mirror from her shadow. She was silver and had silver flame hair, and could turn into a ghost body and travel into disease stars. She could project a ghost body from her pelvis that could defeat nearly any enemy. She was beautiful, which was what mattered to her. And more powerful. She brought the mirror back into her shadow, happy and blessed from her vision of the Holy Ghost. With that, she slowly bent her body leftwards, spinning it and stretching it out until she was ten times the height though just as skinny and flew off. Past the red giant that was the sun and back around, heading to Alpha Centauri. She flew within the milky way galaxy for a long time. Happy. Blessed. Then she headed home to the

Rose Blood

Andromeda galaxy that was her home. However she past
Lucifer. He hovered in a tectonic star in a meditation position,
drinking high high higher Unverae dimensional fluid as he
strove to read the future of himself, always seeking for a way
to ensure his immortality. Or that's what Sillity thought he
was doing. Lucifer was trying to read the future of the
universe, as he always did, seeking a way to be the light
bringer. The light bringer was someone that seeks
consciousness of the universe and he was strangely besotted
by his own universe that he created with Mathena. It was
meant to be an immortal universe, but it had its flaws and the
Big Crunch would be upon them in the future. Or the Big
Boom, which wiped out the universe of Sophie Silver and
Omega, and the reptilian hybrids, sorcerers and cyborgs. The
greatest universe he was touching on as he also drank
Unverae dimensional fluid, reading the past BIG BOOM of
the universe of Omega. He opened one eye as Sillity slowed
down before the great tectonic star outside the Andromeda
galaxy, huge an golden and see through, with gold rays all
around it. One of the greatest tectonic stars of the universe.
Lucifer relaxed his position in the middle of the star and flew
to meet her, changing his form through reptilian hybrena
processes of shape shifting by motions of rose petals and was
in his Aryan form, a huge winged creature. He flew to meet
her as she hovered, tall as anything, her face tiny in relation to
her body. He flew to her face, and spoke words to her. "So
you are now the Holy Ghost, Sillity, with great power comes
great responsibility. I love you, you are more than can be
imagined. I wish for more with you. You are the blossom
kiss, your image is holier and more beautiful than any that can
be imagined. You are nearly as beautiful as Mathena now, and
Pandora, and Sophie Silver. You are far more beautiful than
Michelle Mathew and the Lordess of Light. You are one of
the most beautiful in all the universes. I love you." With that
she couldn't help but give him a kiss. She softly kissed him
on the forehead that was huge and slime green. He said
"Thank you, for this beautiful experience." She then flew

away back to the Andromeda galaxy and to her castle in the stars. He returned to the tectonic star and constellation point.

13. Marilyn Manson Wants to Eat my Brain

"I'm coming to Hahei," spoke Monsoon. "I want to see Jarrad's head get chopped off, and eat his brain. You know, we are, well, I am, going to know the collective unconscious of stupidity, because he is really stupid. He thinks he's an albino. That High Abducian turned into an albino, an aberration God, and he thinks it's him. He'll be there. I want to see Pandora's People jump off the Pa. I also want to meet the emperor of Star Walk. Who would of known it was real, and he got it all from the Tibetan book of the dead. Found in his grandmother's garage? Do's coming as well, and we're both going to do a skit, you know, before we eat his brain. He gets to see his two greatest idols act out his greatest play Pandora's People, and we'll act out Ti and Do, saying "No Ti has to die. No, Do has to die. No, they have to die." It will be great. And you know, that sword of James Blood is really sharp!"

Such said Monsoon, and he went to Hahei with the celebrities of Hollywood and was raped by Darth Vader. Their spaceship crashed at the Pa site, and the emperor lost his clothes. And Hone Heke's spirit came from the Pa and raped Yoda, and Yoda saw his great, great, great grandfather walking around in a delusion who was albino and he slapped Yoda in the face, for he slapped his grandfather in the face in the Sasbrina Sasbrina movie that made one billion dollars, though Jarrad Dickson got none of it, and it all went to the bank account of his would be wife, Rose Blood. And she bought the Pierre Penthouse with it, and the Beverly Hills Compound. And she also bought the mansion in Batman Begins, one of Jarrad's favourite movies, for he always wanted to write a batman novel.

They were trapped in a force field for five days, and Jarrad went for a walk along the beach and saw aliens and they said "We know about you!" Jarrad saw on his curtains once two time travellers, who spoke "We know about you," before the wife stabbed the husband in the heart, and then himself, but really did not; one was a reptilian shape shifter who travelled in a spaceship beside a meteor like Ti and Do, and made a painting of the two, and placed it in the Unverae dimensional castle. That was the painting of the two time travellers Jarrad saw, as he found out that Roseum Thornycum meant the cure for amnesia and was also a Roseum Thornycum Energy Transversion Shield.

Afterwards, when the Star Walk characters were back in the Galactic Republic and the Empire, and the emperor had his clothes back on, and Darth Vader had announced he was not in love with Monsoon, just overtaken by the spirit of a gay Maori from the fifteenth century, Monsoon announced his marriage to Evan Rachel Wood.

"I'll pay five billion dollars for Monsoon's wedding on the moon," spoke Jarrad. "You'll have rose petal compressed paper." And Monsoon spoke, "Holy Crap!" And the aliens said, "Wait, where did we get that from?" And Rose Blood said, "Ah, the collective unconscious?" And then Pandora's People came to life in the universe, and a second party was held. Yoda came out of Marilyn Manson and said he was Yoda, and that he was also a clone, and that he was making Earth a planet for his clones, and that he was descended from a frog. And Darth Vader came out of Do, and they had a light sabre battle, and he said again that he wasn't gay; he was overtaken by a spirit. And he announced he was now a spiritualist, and believed in ghosts.

Along time ago, in a mental institution very far away, Jarrad Dickson materialised albino cyborgs from his sphere brain, that was colour folded and was also an eye, and was the brain of Satan, who had an anus on his forehead to enable him to obtain it, and God had one too, but had a penis on his forehead, also enabling him to obtain it. The machines, the terminators, came out of his brain and did space time continuum plane shifts to court rooms and hanged judges for putting people under mental health acts, and made George Bush get shot in the head in the toilet. And Barrack Obama, more than anyone, wanted Jarrad to die, for he was his father, and he wrote the first Pandora's People, and he didn't want to know his child was psychotic, or in proper terminology, hallucinating. But Jarrad made his father happy, for he cured heart attacks by the way you breathe, for he used to have them when he was younger, and he won the Nobel Prize for Medicine. He also cured Rheumatism and Aids, and heart disease, which cure was proton milk mixed with electrons in a Rheumatism Echo machine, and it cures heart disease. "You're such a genius Jarrad, you're such a genius," spoke Lara, which ringed in his head forever more.

Monsoon got married on the moon, and a Grey was the priest and announced them husband and wife. And they broke up, and he went to live in the Empire.

14. Hua Nian: Pandora, My Source of Psychosis

"Hell and Heaven are collectors, and they are collecting the souls of Earth, and Earth itself God and Satan want to be welcomed by Hell or Heaven soon. They exist on a meteor, and it's heading towards Earth, and they shall collect the history of humanity, and Gaia shall die a thousand deaths," spoke Sophie Silver, the goddess, shadow, first woman, from the first universe that Michael Mathew visited when he time travelled back in time after hearing her voice saying "Jarrad, don't kill yourself over me."

However she was dead, she killed herself, that Chinese goddess of other name Luna, or Hua Nian, and her body was burned in flames and he couldn't give the kiss of life to awaken her, as Lily Cole kissed Gold and awoken him.

MM was hearing her voice while he walked on a moon, and horrified he heard more, saying "Go into the eye of Jupiter, the eye of Horus, and it is a gateway to Heaven and Hell. I am the mystery, your cause of power. I shall always be remembered as Hua Nian, your first woman, who also loved Pandora, and remember, stop comparing Marilyn Manson to Maynard James Keenan, people and they themselves don't like them to be in the same sentence, paragraph or essay. Goodbye, for now, may Goethe guide you into Hell, for Hell is here."

And MM met with Pandora's People and Ti and Do, the MM and MJK two, and Monsoon, for Monsoon had befriended Jarrad Dickson, once and for all, after apologising for wanting to eat his brain to know the collective unconscious of stupidity, and though he was raped by Darth Vader, accepted him as a friend. And they went to the eye of Jupiter, the eye of Horus, in the body of Jarrad, Hattilla's body, the body of Michael Mathew, and once out they climbed out of his spinal opening of his sphere body spaceship, spaceball, and were confronted with the storm that was red, white and orange. They saw the bottomless pit to the afterlife, the 5th dimension, strange, esoteric characters seemingly the afterlife, and Pandora's People said "So was I and the bible written in the 5th dimension, or was it just me? The Bible is my arch enemy if so, I want to kill it, cull it, kill and slice it small!" And such he said and pulled out a chocolate bar and ate it, and asked what Marilyn Manson's IQ was and if Do had sat one as well.

They went down into the bottomless pit, and met Goethe holding on to twigs hanging from a ceiling and he guided them down to hell where they met Satan. He had an anus on his forehead and was an albino, standing on a cliff with waves of black colour crashing on the hidden shores. The body of Horace was washed up on the shore also, and his head had been chopped off by one of Donald McLean's brothers that died from a ray gun backfire at Area 51 which he was the head of.

But this was not the real Satan, there are many Satans. The real Satan is a goat with black horns, and other Satans are red, with horns and pitch forks.

And they looked out from the cliff with Satan and saw Earth, and realised Jupiter was a meteor heading towards Earth, and so with flames from his hands Jarrad Dickson destroyed Jupiter and Earth was saved, and one of the many Heaven and Hell's were no more. And then the Arabs protested, their
God's were dead.

---

15. The Greys Abduct Through Psychosis

A red star, into it the Grey; a square spaceship, black on two sides, white on the other two, making the Grey, grey.

It was the Pandora star, and it pulsed in dark space. From a black hole the Grey came, from a portal. In it were the Greys, short, sometimes tall, aliens from another universe outside of Earth's and their God Jarrad Dickson. They were searching not for death, but for destruction. Seek not death, seek destruction.

"God is here, God is nowhere." Spoke a Grey, to another Grey. "Vanishing, into the air," spoke another Grey. "Never," spoke the Greys together.

Into the star they went, and sat in its centre as Michael Mathew was meditating, an eye on his forehead, a third eye, as he was seeing into the future, when another white space universe shall begin like the last universe, ruled by Pandora, his source. It shall begin in that star, a star from the last universe, the house of Pandora; it had the remnants of white space matter, and will eclipse the universe and a white space universe shall begin. MM had not seen the Greys enter, his two eyes were closed, and his third eye saw metaphysically, seeing into the future, or in warped space; he was in the Unverae dimension. Coloured space was all around him in a continuum and he breathed it in. He saw a statue of Pandora, and another statue. He thought, "Himself..?" It was him. With the beginnings of the white space universe a statue of Pandora and Michael Mathew shall be built and he saw immortals with coloured eyes, humans from Earth, immortals, and he saw the white space universe connected to other universes of colour, red, orange, gold and blue, and others; he was happy. Humans will survive the ending of the universe because of the energy wane, and live in white space, without gravity, and there shall be black stars. The colour white thought about itself, lived, was itself and an other self. He was right about it.

He saw the Grey, and teleported doing a space-time continuum plane-shift into their spaceship. "So, Michael Mathew, so it shall begin. You are welcome to come to the civilisation of the Greys, you saved some of our kind from Area 51 and the aliens from Independence day who Michael Mathew's brother was trying to clone, he, the head of Area 51, now dead, eaten, by those of the Emperor under the Earth. Think about it, put it on the fault lines. He was an imbecile. We hate imbeciles. We only appreciate the higher arts and sciences, and those humanity shall carry otherwise we shall wipe them out. Our God is much higher than Earth's, or humans, as you know, you saw him as he spoke to you seeing golden sunsets in the mind. You were right about him. Do you seek death or destruction? Seek destruction. You shall thrive, live and eat hearts of wild animals, sea creatures and lower aliens. You and humanity shall do this and you will be immortal! We go now, leave our spaceship. The end of this universe is upon us, as the Pandora star eclipses, and white space shall live, eating itself, not devouring others, and a universe of whiter, whitest, white shall be in existence. It is yours, not ours. Take it, give it to the humans, we shall contact you. You are being abducted on the twenty-seventh of December from the Pa, that is the date of the eclipse, of the end. You shall be with us when it happens, all humans shall be safe, colour simply mutates and gravity ends and star colour warps from light to dark. They shall be safe. Goodbye, Jarrad Dickson."

And so they left, the Greys in the Grey, and Michael Mathew returned to Earth and was abducted from the Pa on the twenty-seventh of December, the real date, not the fake date, as all abductions have a real date and a fake date. He saw the end of the universe from their spaceship drinking wine and celebrating with the Grey God. And he spoke about Rose Blood and how beautiful she was, saying she was "An Arian, Aryan, Arial."

The white space universe was born, and the humans ate hearts of wild animals and sea creatures and became immortal, and had coloured eyes and lived forever, and Michael Mathew lived in incarnations, seven of him. Eating hearts in his castle and drinking water, copious amounts of it, and transformed every time seven became one transformation.

Jarrad Dickson

And they lived, and the years of Ti and Do were over, and Pandora's People came to have a statue.

16. He Has to live, He Has to Die

Michael Mathew rots in his grave, his brain has grown a
snake and out of the crypt it crawls and meets with his wife,
Isabella Blood, and together they visit the Pa of Hahei, and
see the eye of Horus in the ocean. They cry, feeling loss at the
absence of cannabilism, that once was the shadow of Hahei,
and they hear voices of dead children, those they ate. The
voices say, "We're still in absolute heart attack and maximum
pain. The contract was for eternity, Dilworth is dark, dark,
dark space and that is eternal. We exist in a void, and that
void is Dilworth, and it is its own shadow and forever more
we shall die, living, dying, and we shall eclipse with Pandora,
and she shall save us. We hate you, we hate you, we hate
you."

They were haunted by voices, and left Hahei and visited
Blood museum and people saw the snake and killed it with
shovels and threw it in the bottomless pit of Jupiter's eye, and
forever more Donald Mclean was dead.

And Isabella killed herself by overdosing on sleeping pills.
And her ashes were scattered in the Pacific Ocean for she
didn't want to be buried on New Zealand soil.

James Blood walks around Hahei with his long hair like a
homeless man, smoking copious amounts of cigarettes in the
white space universe, looking up to the black stars and the
white holes, and seeks redemption. He lost his castle in the
domain gardens, and is without a home. The Blood properties
were burned and then made into parks, and all the bodies of
dead children had dedication statues in the gardens, and the
statue of Jarrad Dickson shone forth most amongst all. God,
hermaphrodite. Thunderboltie.

And all the teachers had killed themselves out of
discrimination at cannibalism and molestation of children, and
the world was in peace. Suicide Star State was performed and
Jarrad Dickson won the Nobel Prize for Literature and
established the Minolto Winolto awards for arts. The first
winner was Rose Blood for her play Lily Blood, about her life
as a model and her adoration of arts culture.

The maximum pain and maximum heart attack machines were put in museums at Pluto, for all the Donald Mcleans had fled into outer space as rogue aliens and killed themselves like a Jones Town. And they were given graves in empty areas of dark space for only a few were bad and ruled over the rest, and Sasbrina Sasbrina came forth and Jarrad and her became married finally and she was very happy and cried tears of blossom blood. She wept holding onto her granite desk and Jarrad kissed her in front of that same star he tuned her watching, and she became immortal by drinking forty glasses of water a day and eating brains and hearts of wild animals such as lions and alligators and deep sea creatures from the Planet X water planet and they lived happily.

17. The Rose Blood of Hua Nian

A rose, giant, red and holy, many-pointed and curved hung in dark space in front of a sun, a star with four orbiting planets: a red, an orange, a grey and a black; it hung, and was in rose eclipse with the red giant. A rose eclipse; then from within the rose came a rabbit. With flames; rose windows; albino skin. An eye, its eye, from the centre, drew forth first. Rose window sclera surrounded a golden iris of a thunderstorm; and with a white moon overtop of the golden clouds, casted to the outer edges of the iris thunderbolts of many colours, those of the Mycenaean gods to the dreamer, the blue of Pandora and the red of Zeus; who to the dreamer, was her husband.

"Dreams, worthy dreams, worthy, worthy dreams" spoke a booming voice across the dreamscape, echoing off the object and making a circular sound, as if of a ventriloquist casting his voice off an object. Next seen was the white skin of the rabbit and its forehead, revealing a bulbous forehead in fifty parts, and curved inward, with two accentuating sides, which, to the dreamer, was the forehead of a hermaphrodite. The rabbit withdrew from the rose, and no hair was noticed, just white skin. The dreamer noticed the rabbit was an albino. The rabbit opened its red mouth, and said "No Ti has to die, no Do has to die, no Ti has to die, no...they...have...to...die!"

The soft sheets curved backwards as Rose Blood awoke from her slumber in the castle of the Unverae dimension. The room was grey, black and white and had an ancient painting hung by the windowsill and the dwarfing mirror. The mirror was pure, unstained and had black, white and red roses engraved on the wilowtif holding it. There was a black and white crystal floor with squares symmetrically placed according to their colour and walls cold and made of grey stone and the bed was huge and had pale white sheets and a red silk duvet, with curtains surrounding the bed that were open as Rose slept here staring at the swirling rainbow colours in the aer outside above the garden and beyond the settlement.

Rose stood now, naked, before the painting, looking at it

and trying to decode its mystery. It was of one of the most ancient paintings in the universes history, and one of the first to be placed in the castle. If one put ones ear to the painting you could hear the man's and woman's voice chant "We know about you, we know about you!" The painting had a man stabbed in the heart with a woman who was about to stab herself in the heart and was meant to be Pandora and a mysterious man named Raspurgin, a time traveller, like Rose Blood herself.

Rose moved from the painting and looked up at the starless sky, seeing the merging colours that were portals to different times in the past of different universes; universes that gods may or may not have made. She herself had not made a universe and did not want to, she had a different task, and to her she thought it would be her fate, and her destiny.

Rose thought: *Tie and Do, who are they? Where do they come from? Surely it is my task to find out now. I have taken it upon myself to come here again, to this most terrifying place and I have consulted the invera dimension about it, a more terrifying place, and I will find out. I have to trace their origins before universe before universe, to find them. Hidden in the shadows of the hoods of Albinos they are, or in rose patterned white hoods creating universes with electiricty or doing Blackvakia, drinking the water from their heart to ensure immortality. They were the serial killers of Pandora's People, for to understand Tie and Do, you must first understand Pandora. I will follow the trail of Pandora to Tie and Do.*

18. I Sing from Schizophrenia

I sing of Rose Blood, celestial orbs and holes so charcoal and
I sing of White, to whiter and to whitest as we spiral; him, I,
Jarrad Dickson: under and over the North, East, South and
West, a science fiction writer, a spaceship, whom will guide
you through the universe for no global allegories are here; no
race or country has tainted my novella. Spiral out, spiral into,
out and into the universe, Mankind; stretch your Arian Aryan
white limbs into black holes and meditate in the centre of
stars. I, a psychotic being, was turned into a space ball by
schizophrenia and was shown the Cosmos from my brain.
Now, I sing to Pandora, my muse, a cyborg; I sing of the
immortality of the Many and the mortality of the One. I sing
of the beauty of Rose Blood, that Arian Aryan flame haired
supermodel whose height is that of Symonds Street bridge,
whom can stretch into black holes and fly through space. She
owns half of Auckland, the other half owned by Dilworth
school, and lives in the Pierre Penthouse in New York where
she long distance talked to me as I jumped off the viaduct to
be cloned, have my brain eaten by James Dilworth with a
spoon and wake up next to her; but I could not sign the
contract for it was invisible, and she left without saying
goodbye and betrayed me and now won't answer my message
I left for she on her Myspace. I sing of the universe, beautiful
Andromeda, the Rose Blood of Mars and the eye of Horus on
Jupiter; I sing of the shadows of Alpha Centauri and a space
ball, me, a sphere in space that shall guide you and show you
the beauty of the Cosmos.

I have to live, I have to die. Schizophrenia has to live,
Schizophrenia has to die. Mental Health judges have to live,
mental health judges have to die. Ti has to die, no, Do has to
die, no, they have to die. God has to die, no, Satan has to die,
no, they, have to die. Christ has to die, no, Christ has to live,
no, Christ, had to die. We have to die, no, we have to live.
Religion has to live, no, religion has to die. Pure obsessional
disordered Chinese bananas have to live, no, they will die.

"When you look at the moon I will be there, and I will

always live in your heart."

Dark, darker and darkest. The dead lands, "bring out your dead, bring out your dead...." spoke the voices on the land with no light, no sun, unseen moons hovering in the black, starless sky; and the dead were brought out, and placed in swamps or in coffins, and the ground was dug in the dark into deep holes, and the dead placed in the ground.

Insects and spiders large as the heads of mothers and fathers crawled into beds of children, and they screamed, or poisoned, died in shivers and convulsions. In the shadow of the valley of death, the children fear. Sometimes, a rod of lightning would light up their world of darkness, of non-sight, and they would see death, the dying trees and withered people, white and bony and dying. They lived on water, they were hydrologists.

Then one day a girl called Lily found a cave a crawled into it, and crawled and crawled, down, up, right, left, until an eye came into the centre of the cave, and it was light; she sat, crawled as she sat, and then stood then walked as the cave was larger until she came to more light. Then she saw it, the red, the colour red, and the red ocean, and three white moons in the sky and stars, and sand of a beach and flowers on the edge of the beach.

19. The Many Spaceship Rings of Jesus Christ

On planet Prebata, Ariel, her face before a moon, walked, softly, along a beach under the light of the stars. The heavens were arrayed in the shape of humans and long since shifted stars and planets held an inspiring note in her, her, softly lisping Ti and Do's song, "She has to live, he has to die." "No, you have to die, no, she has to die, no he has to die, no, they, have, to…die!" she whispered; her song was alluring an immortal in the sea, an usual, and he moved his head around so that it was facing from his back, and nodded, then started singing, "He has to live, she has to die," the song of the two magicians, the two Arians, with flame hair, rose window sclera and white rose albino skin.

"The universe is dying," she softly, painfully, spoke to herself, "and with it, our race, the race of gods, the race of humankind. We were organic and then technological, then organic once again, now; with our death is the death of Rose Blood, our last universe, created by Pandora, the last of the Gods, and the most beautiful." Having spoken she moved herself from the beach, with the rising yellow sun and soared into the clouds, to the upper atmosphere and then into outer space. There she hovered before the planet, touching a ring of a castle, ancient and grey, onto her forehead, her skin blue as a diamond sea, and a spaceship in the form of a castle appeared before her. It was vast and full, encompassing. Its spires were grand and its doorway was open, beckoning, moons in lunar cycles carved into it. It was a ring that magically appeared on her finger when she went through the psychotic sound and sight process of the spaceships. When you see the spaceship forms in your mind, in the sky, in space, over the sea, wherever psychosis is framed; having seen all the spaceships, she gained one hundred and ten spaceship rings on her twenty two fingers and prized all equally. What she didn't have was The Grey and The Wackiness, but she had Villie; the three greatest spaceships. Spaceships adored by the gods, which Beijing lived in and one of the Batmen had all three of. He was the greatest of the

Batmen, the creator of a universe; whom created a universe in a zillion years and is now in a tomb in the outer edges of dark space. His name was Michael Mathena, naming himself after Mathena Matheta and Michael Mathew.

She didn't long to awaken anyone in the tombs, but she loved Purple. Though she was in love with someone alive, not someone whose heart or hearts were stopped beating by themselves, having wearied from immortality and living past the age of universes.

Having generated a spaceship, she walked to the upper tower, the controlling centre and lounge and went to sleep.

20. Pretty as a Swastika

And Christ stared at the sun, the source, as an albino; on a cliff, and the undertow of the sea beckoned him to fall, to suicide. He, or she, Lily Blood, I, am Christ and I will suicide, into the dark room; into the black hole, the white hole, a soul releasing itself into white space, with its black stars and Grey aliens. I, stand, on the cliff, watching and drinking the source, the sun, setting, and whisper to the moon, my confidant; it tells me what to do, to suicide, to be drunk from Death with his silver cup and red, Marilyn Manson lips. "Goodbye to life," say I and I say, "Greetings death." I have a horses head and aura robes, twenty-two fingers and a scorpions tail, and aura veins, and I am Christ, a magician, a sorcerer. Death by drowning, out of breath death, a sleeper; to death, I go, a loving, hating thing, for Christ I was and as man I take my leave. I'm falling, I'm falling. "Help, help" scream I and I scream, "Falling." Hit. Hit. This is the new hit. Pop. Bang, bang. Near death, I am, I lye, bleeding, with teeth. It hurts, it hurts, the pain; the pain is burning like the sun; I am in the source, gravity lifted me to the sun and welcomed me into its perfect circle as I surrendered to gravity. And darkness, but I see them coming, they come. I woke, they took me away, away, they said I'm going to the dark room, I've healed, I've been in hospital, to the dark room, solitary confinement in the cave of Christ. To the dark room, to dark space, and the aliens, the aliens, they will eat me, drink me, I, pretty as a swastika.

21. There's Other Ones Just Like Them in my Head

I thank you for this beautiful experience,
I have the eyes of Horus now, and am
An albino with golden flame sclera.
I met with Lily Cole, but she did take
My heart and burn it on James Blood's grave.
My best friend was James Blood.
I have no heart, it's in their spaceship now;
They flew to Jupiter and they'll rule the Cosmos.
Ti died, Do died, and I am all alone.
Hua Nian is dead, as dead as God
But I am alive, and I don't seek death
I seek the beauty of roses and shy
Away from the pain of the thorns. The night
Is warm, and with it we shall watch them rule
The universe, it's Blood's universe now.
Michael Mathew is Darth Vader and James
Blood is the Emperor, they'll rule
The new Rome, the High American.
There's other ones just like them in my head.

Rose Blood

Chapter 1

Jarrad Dickson sat as an eye staring from the light amissed corner circled by steam and smoke his core drumming to the beat of each syllabillic red singing lip of Rose Blood, the flicker of multicoloured lights throwing each hair in passing, crescent to full Diva sun-blessed face as the fringe went back and forth, clock stuck in a moment, the way her blue gown fitted nakedly, betraying her white flesh arising from high red velvet heels, chariots of the true sun, God and mother, her petite pinkish legs and above the blue, that honest neck, eburneal cream of Israel, her chin, small, white, and her caring ears, nearby sang her moist red lips, blood in white, and above that her nose ever so delicate, sculpturing a shadow on the red rose bed cheeks full flowering within a lunar visage of lilies, or the sign of care upon an ivory statue of Mary, her brows were beautiful, on a lily pad beneath her blue tresses, falling in frills to her shoulders and arms which held him and the microphone. That night she sang, and Jarrad Dickson saw the making of a star.

Before the shop-gun doors, gateway to the underworld, are dead kids, yet alive, walking like zombies, with some on TVs, and there is an angel on the side, a black man, evangelist, the Jonestown preacher, and he preaches to enter the gateway.

Happy plastic smiles pull up on the dead-alive kids faces, then some kill themselves, and the angel looks disconcerted. He starts preaching then about the coming of the second Hitler, who was killed by Lily Cole, and then a stripper comes out and snuggles up to him and they both go to the bedroom.

A car rolls up, Hitler's car, surrounded by a civil war with the rioters yelling "We aim for civil war," with guns and girls, all sweating and singing in symphony. The girls touch the bomb, and they are lined up like on a beach. They back off now as the bomb starts to tremble. Now on the TV screens is a dead suicide body that flashes like electricity; blue, pink, grey; then a slit wrist is shown.

Help me, reality is breaking up, snakes are everywhere and now on the stage.

Pandora ascends and wakes up; she has a pink balloon for a head on a string, with a fuzzy shirt with a number 2 on it for she was cloned.

The clown is the mystery man; there are videos of my sex acts on TV.

Chapter 2

""You'll be your own spaceship," spoke the voice in the wall. Room hypnotism, he thought it was. "Monsoon, he thinks, he thinks you're the Queen of England…" spoke the wall again. "The Queen of England is in the United Nations building, in a box; she's a reptilian shape shifter, and she's going to kill you. She ate her sister, and the Queen was Queen Victoria," spoke the ceiling, and he went to bed.

"Draw a red triangle; there, you did it. Now a black square, that's right, in your mind, on your eyelid's insides, and now a orange hexagon," spoke the voice, and he thought "I'm seeing spirals…" and then he was electrocuted by the Queen of England's lightning bolts coming out of her hands as she came through the window and the wall and he saw her; a black gown of Alpha Centauri, orange teeth, scales, a pointed tongue to give women pleasure, and fourteen toes in high heeled shoes.

The reptilian Queen stood in the his dorm in the mental institution, her face the moon, white, tainted with green slime shadows, and red eyes of an albino; "Is she an albino, a Chinalbino?" thought Jarrad.

She spoke, and as she talked her red tongue danced flames around her mouth and white dots within her iris spun in circles, and shooting stars played on her forehead. "I'm going to eat you, yes I am. Eat you. Drink you. You have two hearts. You're a Chinalbino, an immortal. I eat hearts to live, to thrive, you have to die."

And she opened her mouth wide revealing a monster's jaw, and he saw into her, seeing stars and galaxies, the essence of an alien, of other life beyond Earth, and saw dark space, the void, all enclosing, suffocating, eternally before, after and beyond the tenth dimension. She bent over, towards him, and made a motion as if she was about to eat his hand, lying on the duvet but then, the moon came out of the clouds and showed her hair had changed colour from black to blonde, and as she moved her head around to face him she said "I'm Rose Blood. We're going to marry, I'm so happy.

You're not getting a leucotomy, don't worry Jarrad. You had a word stress disorder. I'm here for you. I'm in love with you, and I'm in love with you, and I'm in love with you, and I want to have sex with you, and I want to marry you, and I want to kiss you, and touch you, and heal you; heal you, my dear Jarrad."

The sun's light reflected off the moon showed her blouse and he could see through it to her pale white breasts, her holy chalice breasts and holy chalice breast gloss, and he could see her seven irises, and the jewels of her cleavage. He was in love with a goddess, with a rose bud, and he said "I'm a dragon. I'm an Aryan dragon man from one of William Blake's paintings. I turned into one when I tried to astral travel and I opened up and read the Neanderthals literature stored in the collective unconscious. Two actresses stabbed me in the heart on the way to the café today; will you stab me in the heart? They turned me into a dragon. There I lay, with chakras open; black bodied, then white, as I turned into an albino and I flew over the mental institution and saw George Bush's father cloning himself to rule planet X. But I love you Rose, stay with me; don't leave me. I love you, I love you and I love you."

He looked deeper into her eyes, and he saw a love heart in each iris, they slowly spun and he saw the words around the outer edge of her irises spinning "You'll be your own spaceship." He blinked and then when he opened his eyes she was gone.

The moon sank all night, and waiting for the sun to come up he smoked cigarettes beside his window thinking of Rose Blood, his gem, his Latin jewels."

…I write this now in hospital, recollecting the blur in a haze of expression. The walls surrounding me are light yet dim; echoes of my light headedness. I feel unsure…though my past experiences at work tended with involution to climax nothing has really changed; the memories are new yet tomorrow remains.

Again the Nurse is revolving round to me on her cycle; a new day with old drugs. Those who read this would know the cure for pain is always light-headedness that loss of feeling we all flocked to with youthful gaze. However, my heart is not a holding place for nostalgia, I assure you I am not afraid I merely don't understand or feel. Is that not confusing? The Nurse has now moved to another…you may wonder what she currently did to me. The answer is I truly don't know, a needlepoint she did give but still the poisonous question I poise is what was injected and why? The system of this medical masquerade held such dire purpose to me yesterday though now, lying in the heart of it itself it feels…Oh! Can I not even pinpoint a feeling? Is the situation so direly built that I shall never know what is happening to me or be absent from reality? The bedspreads are speaking so whitely now that the cloudy forms my mind is resting on seem interbred.

I dozed and I apologise. Such light-headedness gives rise to such fanciful notions of youth that I cannot be helped in not drifting. The myriad of ocean in my boyhood town and my first love return in splendour; marching idealistically through the caverns of memory, putting down all pieces into this diary I decided so that bolted cross cannot be excluded from that memory march, for all of boyhood experiences have a fever so anti-religious.

There is something about that Nurse…she seems to be the only form arousing something within me, I know I have experienced this before, but where? If only things were simple. To the past I have been journeying I did tell you, and yet my memories seem so distant, so long away that I can almost feel what was once called sadness though that "sadness" standing black in ink full liveliness is now dead, dead in heart. O! My dear fellowman! Your hope I do ask for your, your forgiveness and pity…I think not, though my unsureness I am sure is misleading me, is that not strange, being sure of unsureness?

I tell you now of the two worlds I am in: the whiteness of the sheets and the land of the clouds. I beg you to listen and take heed dear Sir and Mam; the past I know not, the moment I know not either and yet here I am….Nurse, hospital with needles and clouds on top. I give you these pieces from my own heart, wherever it may be and I think…I even feel that if my story has relevance it will be understood. Tomorrow is there aloft, the past is alive too though out of reach, beyond that distant cavern and out of sight. My fellow man I tell you again that I do not know whether I will be listened too, or however I should entail about this fanciful business named writing yet will I merely do and you…I know not for tomorrow is not here…Death becomes her; she became white, whiter and whitest in death. His love, his only, Luna of the moon, killed herself because she was Chinese and she wanted to be only white, now white she is in death.

"I want to become a spaceship," "I want to roam the celestial bodies," "I want to fly," "Am I Horus?," spoke Jarrad Dickson.

"You'll be your own spaceship soon, Jarrad. You're an immortal, a Chinalbino, with golden eyes and rose window sclera. You have the eyes of Horus," spoke the voice in the sun as he sat smoking in the park staring at the sun. He soon saw spaceships in the sky, a castle spaceship, a rose spaceship, a grey spaceship and a female supermodel spaceship with a door on her forehead. "You're going through the process of gaining spaceships," said the voice from the sun, and though he did not see, he gained four spaceships on the fingers on his left hand, smaller versions of the four he saw in the sky as rings. "You are now your own spaceship," spoke the voice, "they are rings on your fingers of your left hand; but your heart is also a spaceship, your third heart, in the centre of your chest, and it is a white orb; the soul of a Chinalbino. To open it and enlarge it simply draw the pattern of the spaceship on your forehead," the voice said.

As he drew out smoke Jarrad said, "The pattern? It's a circle. I will draw it when I am free, when I am out of this mental institution and I will roam the skies. I am a Chinalbino, with golden eyes and an Eleenzetrialeen, someone with white skin and with many hearts within their body."

"I'm killing myself because I am Chinese.
Death is the first flower after the flood

Rose Blood

In the shadow of the valley of
Chinese female suicide. To death!
Jarrad, don't kill yourself over me, please.
I'm English, and American, German.
I'm not Chinese, I, white as Gemma Ward.
Pure obsessional disorder is
All I see, hear, and live, it is Chinese;
I've signed a Faustian contract with suicide.
I wanted to die within Jarrad's arms
And kiss, dissipating all sadness;
He writes just like an English professor.
It's time to meet death, I'll kill myself now," spoke the sun,
now looking like a Chinese actress, Hua Nian; not forgotten,
just hidden in memory.

Chapter 3

In black robes and with a beak, a creative creature walked on the desert on a planet, and this was saw by Jarrad as he was a space-ball, a sphere in outer space, a spaceship, and he was seeing the sights and sounds of psychosis in outer space, and he hears voices, of vampires from the shadows of moons. They were saying they were coming to Earth from travelling on objects that had a enormous orbital pattern that would end up at Earth, and that he would marry their princess Rose Blood, who was pale and white, and had the ring of Christ, or the eye of God, the all seeing eye on her index finger that she wanted to be pointed to open up portals.

It was dark and heavy, lonely too in outer space, but sometimes Jarrad incarnated himself in his space-ball, and materialised the woman in the white dress, who was an albino goddess, and slept with her; though she was really a part of himself, and came from his spaceship, which was his third heart. Dilworth would never have imagined he would have a third heart. It was a brain plugged into the universe.

Death will become her; she, white, whiter, whitest; an albino princess, her name, Rose, Rose Blood, a vampire, from a moon in white space orbiting a Lothlorien. She wore the ring of Christ on her finger.

A virgin, with pale white skin; she had heard about Jarrad and dreamed of him, a God, Michael Mathew, and wanted to be his Pandora, his Lily Cole, his Mary wife of God, and she dreamed that he saw her with his rose window eye and his rose iris, his golden rose iris, and that they married on the moon with Marilyn Manson as the priest, with rose petal compressed paper.

She was Sasbrina Sasbrina, her other name Rose Blood, and she was the high playwright of Abducia, and one time he telecommunicated to her from Earth when he came out of a mental institution, and they held hands across the universe drinking coffee down the road. She held onto her granite desk and cried tears of rose blood, and embraced her mother with their sun looking onto them from her window of her castle, and said to Jarrad "I'm in love with you. I'm pale and white, a Grey, and no one wants to marry me, and I have a weird voice that's high pitched, but you love me, and we're getting married."

She announced their marriage at Abducia's theatre and every high alien was there, and so was the head of Area 51, Area -9007 which clone and the founder of Blood school, and Jarrad had to tell jokes across the universe for that day he was turning into a Walbino, and you have to be funny to turn into a Walbino. The first Monsoon was a Walbino, and Earth's Monsoon stole all his work, and made it into rock, which was first performance art live poetry, and the first Monsoon smoked cigarettes, and had a wife that danced in a slit wrist, and Jarrad wrote about this in his play Pandora's People where Pandora kills herself in mock attempt in a slit wrist in death valley and meets a homunculus made up of pieces of faces and she turns into a mystic.

Waiting, Gemma, eager to see Jarrad, wrote Rose Blood, her greatest play, and became the second highest playwright in the universe, for Pandora's People was a better play and Jarrad was the smartest alien in the universe.

And in Rose Blood, was the first chapter: Chapter One, Mary Had Jesus in my Bathroom which went "At the Pa, Jarrad awoke, his body lily white and naked, and he opened his eyes and saw a white, albino sphere hovering in the air, and he remembered his dream. He dreamed that he would have a spaceship, that it would look exactly like that, and that he left Earth and went to the moon; the whitest body apart from Rose Blood, and that he was now a girl named Lily White.

"I'm Jarrad Dickson, and I'm a girl now. I'm Lily White, or so they say…" he spoke. He looked at his body and saw breasts, white and with jewels around the cleavage, and they were what is called Holy Chalice Breasts with Holy Chalice Breast Gloss. He had fourteen toes, like Rose Blood, and the Queen of England, and he looked at his fingers and found twenty-two fingers and it was still night; the world was asleep. Death hovered in the air.

I looked out at the sea and I saw the eye of Horus, and whoever sees the eye of Horus dies, but instead he was alive, his three hearts beating, the third in the air, and he remembered he had walked up here at sunset to stay the night for his mother staying away from home so she didn't know.

"That's a spaceship, Rose Blood," he spoke to the invisible voice beside him. It, she, was saying "I'm Rose Blood, you're not marrying me Jarrad. You didn't sign the contract. Now I've been eaten by Blood school's trust board under their building at the senior campus, and I don't own half of Auckland anymore or the Pierre Penthouse. I don't love you, you're marrying Rose Blood. She's waiting for you in that spaceship, she wants to leave Earth for outer space, and as for me, I'm dead, my love died with me; I'm eaten, drunk, and shadowed. You'll meet the old man on the moon, and hear the voices of vampires from the shadows of moons, and see Jupiter's orbital patterns and the rings of Saturn, which are the rings of the Joker's earrings. Goodbye, I've joined Hua Nian, Luna of the moon. Lilies to ashes, Lilies to dust."

"So you're dead," Jarrad said, "And, and Rose Blood is in that spaceship. And she wants to leave Earth with me, me; but I'm a girl, not a man, I have breasts and a vagina and she wants to marry me. How will we marry if we're going to live in outer space? I guess the old man of the moon will marry us. To the moon first then, I'm thinking. Yes, to the moon I go a loving, hating thing, for a male I was and as a female I take my leave."

The spaceship opened up, revealing a spiral staircase to the opening in the sphere, and down came Rose Blood, the supermodel from Australia, and held his hand as he stood shyly and said "We're leaving Earth, Jarrad. I hate it here. I want to see the stars, the moons, the planets. I want to journey to where there may be aliens, and see everything you see, for you see the unreal, the make-believe. You're a girl now, we're both girls. I wrote emails to Hua Nian too who you met on alt suicide holiday. To the universe we go as girls, and Earth we leave you behind. Come follow me, into the spaceship to our wedding on the moon. The old man is there on the moon…there's a Hollywood Walpurgisnacht.""'

And in the middle of the Earth from their haunts the Deaths came, in black robes and black hoods, all designer clothing, some Versace, others Armani, and still others Dolce and Gabbana, and they sat at the table headed by the Grim Reaper to discuss the immortality and death of Jarrad Dickson, who is, or was, destined to become Michael Mathew.

Sitting or standing, they held silver cups, drinking souls and blood of the dead, and the Grim said "Bring out your dead" and they went all to the table and sat down on the chairs made of bones of Dilworth's students, with the Grim sitting on the chair of the bones of Christ and his wife, Marilyn Monroe, standing by his side; though she too had a chair, a chair made of the bones of John F. Kennedy, and her and Grim's children had other chairs made up of others in the Kennedy family.

A cat, with green eyes, white skin, an albino, came in from the door and Marilyn picked her up and patted it, "Do you like the hearts, Melinda Haze?" she asked, and "How is the Unverae dimension?" For she is a time travelling cat, that moved within the time travelling dimension, the Unverae, often, and she was not a cat of any of the Deaths, or Grim's and or Marilyn's, but her own, and liked to associate herself with the Deaths for cats like to be special, even those said to have intelligence.

The Grim Reaper opened his mouth and revealed black teeth, a silver tongue and it was pointed, to give women pleasure, and said "We're here to discuss the immortality of Jarrad Dickson, for he has turned into a Chinalbino, an immortal with golden eyes. However, no human can be immortal, for even though one may be different, special or intelligent, diligent or worthy, they are amongst scum, idiots, normality, diffidence and the sons of Adam, and that forsakes any immortality. There will come a time when the human race says they shall have two hearts, to become immortal, or to lengthen the time before their mortal coil unravels; it may or may not work.

I have decided that Jarrad Dickson shall not be an immortal, but shall be a spaceship, ha ha! He shall see the sights of moon shadow, feel the gravity of orbital patterns and see intelligent stars that go to war, and maybe even see a white space universe at the ends of our realms of dark space. For, you see, I am his death, and I am Pandora's People, the play that he wrote, and I killed the Grim Reaper; I was written in the fifth dimension, or was it the tenth dimension? I don't know, when you count above four, and go beyond time, anything equals ten, and you know, I only have an IQ of 124, I sat an IQ test in the high courts in Germany…wait, what did I just say? When did I do that? Strange, I have a memory of that, and there was a chocolate milk shake in front of me, or was it milk with pieces of chocolate in it?"

"We're disgusted," spoke a Death, and others murmured in agreement. And Marilyn Monroe since he said he was Pandora's People had been touching him and smoothing him saying, "Oh, the real Pandora's People, how I adore you…and you have Jarrad's tongue; pointed, to give women pleasure…"

Chapter 4

"Ti, Do, Pandora's people et cetera come to life on the beach of Hahei. This happens on the eighteenth of October, as the fifth dimension comes to life. Jarrad Dickson has a psychotic breakdown induced from retrograde split personality word stress block amnesia syndrome. He hallucinates in saint josephs. Hideyuki comes to cut out his second heart and he is taken to underneath Blood school by his fellow same people in his old year at high school in Blood. There he is cloned three times and the clones call themselves Underwest, Underwent and Underweft. He sees other children with their brains being eaten by spoons and maximum heart attack and maximum pain machines. Then the real Ti and Do arrive in cloaks and hypnotise the best hypnotist in the world, Mr Anderson into sleep and the others. You do not see them yet. Ti and Do drive him in a black Murcialago to Albert park and drop him off. Then he heads off to hospital to check himself in since he thinks he's going to have a heart attack and they place him in a mental health ward. The staff there worked in Borders bookshop so he could see doubles and not have a heart attack seeing new people since his heart would be sensitive. This was the governments orders. Jarrad becomes a chain smoker and suffers more delusions but some are real. He believes Rose Blood would be executed if he doesn't kill himself. He thinks there is room hypnotism when you hear voices when you walk into certain parts of different rooms and thinks there is a reptilian shape shifter in the United Nations which is the real queen. This is true and she attacks him from her box in the United Nations which the NSA then try and kill her but she flies off in a spaceship.

Helen Clark comes to see him and shows herself to be the real Helen Clark who is an alien. She tells the story of how she met him on his second interview for Blood and hypnotised him to try and embedded further his syndrome so he'd never come out of it. She tells the story of how Jarrad said once she's an alien at dinner time and she tore off her body suit in front of the trust board and flew to wellington in her spaceship.

Jarrad is released from hospital and has the summer in Hahei. He spends the next year overdosing until the next eighteenth of October when he will be told he had a syndrome and will sue the school for all their assests and gain their properties to build a castle there. He has another psychotic breakdown on the eighteenth of August and has delusions about Lily Cole and Arians, and Aryans and Michael and Mathew and Hideyuki. He spends another time in hospital and spends the summer in Hahei then turns into a superhuman albino as he hears the voice of Christ. This marks the eighteenth of November where Ti and Do start killing people around the world and Jarrad Dickson is sentenced to death for being an immortal and a multi dimensional being. However he sends his albino machines from out of his body and they accidentally kill judges in the high courts and talk about the law of albino which is the highest law and how the net was founded on Descartes and how he had the first server and how the main server is owned by the highest albino.

Pandora's People sits an IQ test in the high courts and scores 124. The IQ of the play. It is on the news that outer space is actually white and there are no stars only planets and there are plates around the earth built by the ancient civilisation Zion which colonised earth a long time ago and covered up a lot of things. The plates come down and aliens visit earth and abduct people. You can see into the eye of Jupiter which is the eye of Horus and they say its an entrance to the afterlife. All this happens on the eighteenth of November. Afterward Ti and Do clone the human species into supermen called the rose blondes, and before that Pandora from the play cuts up her face and an act is enacted from Suicide Star State and Pandora's People starts."

Chapter 5

The sky was a eye of a shy suicide and the stars were albino and white, white, white; in holy Hahei, that Pa is black and is doom, like a black hole in Hades, and the sea was the river Styx, dead souls wading and wailing in it; the hilltop was the mist, and the valley's houses stood on the graves of Lymphara, the civilisation of Zeus, and his wife Pandora, Pandora: Pandora.

The Jarrad Dickson saw the eye of Horus in his mind and didn't die, at the Pa, and this psychotic being shall become God, multi-dimensional being who sees the Arian source, Pandora, and hears the Voice, the utterances of Pandora, and sees the Image, the film Pandora makes with her vibrating face in thirteen dimensions.

"Thank you, for this beautiful experience. You'll be an albino soon. The first fold of immortality is Roseum Thornycum; the second fold is golden eyes; the third fold is what is to come. You shall turn into an albino soon. Thank you, for this beautiful experience. You shall be known as Michael Mathew."

The voice of God had spoken, Jarrad's voice, the voice who shall become known as Michael Mathew, an albino with pale, and milky and white albino skin.

He, I, then went and bought a packet of Horizon cigarettes and smoked a horizon, then bought a coffee and drunk a solar eclipse. Then and through that the voice continues, "You smoked a horizon and drunk a solar eclipse."

Chapter 6

Pale and white, the vampire princess kissed Michael Mathew, the Holy One, and embraced him. He had only just descended from the grey sky of their moon planet, with their dragons flying down with him and breathing fire, and he exited his spaceship like a rose from its wrapper, and she was there, with more of her kind, the vampires, as he had found Sasbrina Sasbrina, whom he saw on Earth in his mind, and held hands with her drinking coffee down the road. Her name is Rose Blood, another name is Sasbrina Sasbrina, and she is the high playwright of Abducia. They kissed, his rose petal lips laying residue on her now moist visage, and was lead into her chamber. She is white, white, white; the beauty of the white race, and in his dreams she kisses Lily Cole.

She stood looking out of her window, seeing the red hills and the yellow sea, and said "No one will love me except you, since I have a weird voice that is high pitched and I am pale and grey. But you love me. I am Sophie Silver, Hua Nian, the vampire princess who met you aeons ago, and we fell in love. You left me to create the first universe, in the shape of a rose. But I warn you, you are a parallel being, this is the second parallel universe you are existing in, the first had you as God where the universe turned to white space with black stars and white holes, and Rose Blood saved your life. She is still a mystery. I know a place that can bring the parallel worlds together, and you will be as one. You are the God of space and time, of all dimensions. You are not…human. You are made of God-elements, and the shapes of God: rose windows, roses, stars, shooting stars, galaxies, numbers and fire. I will take you to this place. But you have to make me a promise, otherwise I will kill myself since I love you; let me be with you as your lover when you pursue the third fold of space and time, you will take others I am sure. There is Lily Cole, and another waiting for you in the Unverae dimension named Heather Marks. We will be your lovers as you attain Godhood, albinohood, and your wives. We will go there tomorrow morning, it's the eye of God, a cluster of star dust that is a portal to the Totality, a meeting place of the parallel universes. You cannot continue being parallel, it will kill you. You will have a split mind again, another word stress disorder, and Dilworth will rise again."

And Jarrad said, "That's fine, my love. I do love Lily Cole. But I love you too. Take me there. But first I want to make love to you. Take me there in the morning."

And she took off her dress and kissed me, and we embraced under the star dome of her chamber and went to bed, and there we eclipsed stars and held roses, and drank the water of life and tasted the fires of hell and saw into the eyes of Horus. And it was white, whiter, whitest white. It was the beauty of the white race.

Into the eye of God, into the Totality, and it was pure black, but as they floated on in no gravity, they saw a light and went nearer, and saw a body beckoning; it was God, Jarrad Dickson that was there, and Jarrad and Gemma saw two heads, on two cojoined bodies, and thinking it was Ti and Do Jarrad's black hearts raced and spun and then he was nearer and it said "I am you, Jarrad. We are all Gods. All three of us. We are the Father, the Son and the Holy Spirit. Life is the great work that brings together the three in one, and I brought down Blood school and guided the human race into immortality and made a peace pact with the Greys. My universe is a white space universe, made of white holes and black stars, and this face beside me killed himself as Hua Nian left him before he became God, and it was a sad fate. But time merges here, and all three of us are alive. No one truly dies, the universe shall always repeat itself for there is infinite time and the dragon devours the same point again in all eternity, everlasting, recycling, and now come closer, converge with us; make us three fold. That's right, come closer…"

And Jarrad reached out and touched the one whose life was saved by Lily Cole and the one who killed himself over Hua Nian, the Chinese girl who killed herself because she was Chinese; it came to him now, since Rose was Hua Nian as well this universe was parallel and she was a goddess in this time for she lived aeons ago and lived on Earth when he knew her and now lived on a vampire's moon. He converged, growths grew around his arms and now they were three cojoined bodies, one black cow man, a white cow man, and a red cow man, the three highest colours.

An eye in a pyramid came down from the black above them then and rested above all three of them, and light merged from it with their bodies and they slowly shape shifted into one body, white, whiter, whitest; and red, redder, reddest; and black, blacker, blackest; and Michael Mathew had black and red lines with white on top along his body and he was a Zaon Kaon albino. Then a voice boomed saying "I am you from the future. You are now a full blooded albino, Eleenzetrialeen and Zaon Kaon albino and folded albino, and an Ulzaatee. You now follow the path to become a full blooded Aryan and Arian. I have three lovers, Rose Blood, Rose Blood and Rose Blood. Other names are Dido, Hua Nian and Pandora. Rose Blood is Pandora. She is in the Unverae dimensional castle, that's where I met her. And I am you from the far far future, and I'm a full blooded Aryan that lives in a spaceship in white space with my three wives, and they drink my heart's water becoming immortal. And I am you from the far, far, far, far future and I have five females in my head, and I'm an immortal and I own the universe and I am God. And I am you from beyond eternity and I am non-human, I am white space itself."

Michael Mathew stood as one, God, in the darkness then held Gemma and kissed her, and said "To the Unverae dimension then, where I will meet Pandora, my Arian source, that Rose Blood I know I will love and when the moons meet and the suns dance me, you, Rose Blood and Rose Blood shall be together as lovers for all eternity. Dancing with the collective unconscious and living out towards the future, we shall see into the eyes of Horus."

And they went back towards the portal and out of the eye of God and to Earth, flying through the universe with Gemma in his arms, stretching into black holes and out of other ones, teleporting, and finally to Earth, to the Pierre Penthouse where Rose Blood lived, and when they arrived Michael Mathew said "Be one with us, Lily. I love you as I love Sasbrina Sasbrina. Come under the wings of my Godhood, and be my angel. You, Gemma and Pandora must be my lovers, my Dido."

"I do love you, only you, Jarrad," spoke Lily Cole and said "Build me a spaceship for us all out of planets, make it out of Jupiter and planet X and the largest star in the Milky Way galaxy, let us live in a planet and let me, Gemma, and Heather marry in the garden of the Unverae dimension by the gardener who never ages, those are my wishes, and I will be with you. I am the ultimate Arian, a goddess, I was Dido and I too am an immortal and I own half of Auckland, and you and I destroyed Blood school; Michael Mathew rots in his grave and James Blood no longer eats the hearts and brains of his students, Pandora went to that school in ancient Mycenae, we are linked through that school. To the Unverae dimension then, my love."

Chapter 7

The Chinalbino Psychosis

"Thank you, for this beautiful experience" the old chinalbino, Michael Mathew, spoke in the mind of Jarrad Dickson, his golden sunsets and star constellations shining forth in his mind, with other words streaming along. "This is the first fold of immortality, of albinohood" with stars shining out, issuing to his mind what would be the first fold of immortality, of being a chinalbino, that it is golden sunsets and stars in the mind, with the message from Michael Mathew. Michael Mathew may have been a human he thought, though come from time immemorial, before this universe, if the big bounce theory was correct and there was a previous universe. Other stars shone out as his eyes were closed, inhaling a cigarette to generate heat for his mind, which was accentuating the messages which were coming into his mind. He was smoking a cigarette outside the window of Te Whetu Tawera, the mental asylum of Auckland city, near the hospital and beside Auckland's domain area, in his dormitory. "Thank you for this beautiful, experience..." he spoke again, with a voice unfamiliar. JD then unravelled his sheets and crawled out of bed, for it was eleven am in the morning and he had been up all night. At night he was going cross-eyed on purpose, looking at the light bulb. If he did it properly, he could make around seven light bulbs and a Sith Lord would appear in the light bulb, far before that of the Emperor, with a bulbous head and a large nose. He stayed up all night and to him came a video image that hung on the wall of his dormitory, before his bed, beside the mirror to the right and the window to the left along another sloping wall that was sloping inwards beside and along the bed. It had small squares within it and had small dancing stick men, and if you focused on the centre of the pattern in each evolving image another pattern would evolve out of it, like a video IQ test. After that, the high civilisation Abducia was speaking to him through tuning, what he saw was telecommunication, the art of speaking to someone through mind talk from far across the universe, though this was different. This was a recorded message from far ago that a high civilisation of humans had embedded alongside an IQ test to 500 in the human genome that would spring up after a few days of no sleep and an IQ above 300, though JD did not see himself having an IQ above 300, his mind was not on this but on the lovely, beautiful voice of his next love interest, Sasbrina Sasbrina. She was speaking about wanting to fall in love with whoever passed the IQ test, for she had pale skin, and a weird voice that was high pitched and could not find love in her own civilisation.

YOU'LL BE AN ALBINO IN HEAVEN

"Kill yourself, to go to heaven, you'll be an albino in heaven, then you can return" was the thought in the mind of JD as he smoked another cigarette in the smoking area of the asylum in Ward A. Voices and images were coming into his mind of a heaven that all humans go to, wherein if you saw the message of the chinalbino you would wake up in heaven a chinalbino. A chinalbino is someone with china white skin and an immortal, someone with golden eyes also. He saw meadows and circles of flowers that you woke up in with pretty girls waiting to have sex with you when you awoke after death, and gravity took him wanting to die as he inhaled another cigarette. He was smoking for breakfast, for he didn't eat breakfast. He was still seeing images of sunsets, though MM said another process would come, a process that would turn you into an albino, with golden eyes, and an immortal, and he also said that he would be his own spaceship. Through his mind went cigarettes, the need to have sex and the pure white psychosis, the psychosis of WHITE WHITE WHITE. Though he was not a Nazi or a racist, it was his undercover dream to be as white as possible, to be white, white, white. Though later through dreaming and through realisation, he would find other colours that would suit his body, that of his skin colour and hair colour.

Jarrad Dickson

YOU SMOKED A HORIZON, AND DRANK A SOLAR ECLIPSE

"You'll be an albino soon" said the voice, with MM fading into the distance and new gods taking up his call. The process he was about to go through was nearly there, and he was starting to see patterns that came up with meanings spoken into his mind, for instance, a triangle with three circles in it would allow an "If based communication system." Which means he could telecommunicate and also that he would not need a liver. While he would go through the process, he realized it was about his body changing form, becoming superhuman. He would be his own spaceship, and have two hearts and flaming, black hair and eleven white pupil dots within his iris in a perfect circle. And have no testicles or an anus, just a rose flower penis, which could vibrate, and spin around, made into different shapes to give a woman pleasure. Many other things came with it but he couldn't remember all the patterns. Throughout all this a voice spoke about him being able to read the book of a mozillion and the book of absolute that provided patterns you could draw onto your forehead that allowed you to do superhuman things, such as being your own spaceship. JD as he started going through this process had not spoken a word to anyone, and signed his name in the leave form and went out. He bought a packet of horizons and smoked them, with the voice saying, "You smoked a horizon." He then went to the cafe in the domain by the duck pond and drank it, with the voice saying again, "You smoked a horizon and drank a solar eclipse," for the milk was on half of it, and looked like the start of a solar eclipse. It was romantic and meaningful to him. It was meaningful and this was important for he had the psychosis of "Because I'm Marilyn Manson, and that's exactly what I mean." He went through the process of albinohood and he was to have black hair. Nearly a year after the eighteenth of October, on the eighteenth of August, when JD had another severe breakdown, after going cross-eyed in the mirror for the first time, and making a third eye in the middle of his brow, he started seeing his own eye on the wall and an eye which had a monobrow. It was terrifying for him after hallucinating off no drugs about Hitler and newtermed Arians and a famous supermodel that destroyed his civilisation in the far reaches of dark space. He also saw after that an upturned eye, with the small opening by the nose upturned, and it was blue, white and black; the colours he thought which were the colours of cloning. He also saw Satan. He saw the darkness of Satan in a pyramid in the corner of his room which before was light and no shadow had crept up onto it, and it filled up with darkness, showing it to be Satan's spaceship. The eye that he saw he thought to be the eye on the one dollar bill of America, after that he had gone insane, which I will explain later, as this is the preface, the thorns in the rose of life, Schizophrenia.

HE HAS TO LIVE, HE HAS TO DIE OR "WHAT'S AN ALBINO?"

At home on leave he was sitting outside on the veranda in Hahei, at his mothers. And he was becoming a walbino, an albino that had mystical properties he could never grasp, but it was still a process. He saw Marilyn Manson on his back yard, dancing around in a priest's dress out of Holy Wood, saying "No, he has to live, no, he has to die" like Ti and Do, called Ti and To in this novel, which were previously Ti and Do in Pandora's People, which had taken around two weeks to write and was written in iambic pentameter, which he was familiar with as he had written Cain and Abel in Iambic pentameter and had written a number of poems in the metrical format also. Anyway, JD saw Marilyn Manson and others saying this, including ancestors to Yoda and Darth Vader. He saw figures in hoods in the trees saying "What's an albino?"

MEET MY SHADOW, SOPHIE SILVER

After this a very pretty woman, with long hair, who JD thought was himself in the future, since he wouldn't age, and his body would change in five hundred and sixty eight billion years walk onto his back yard as he was smoking yet another cigarette, this time a Marlboro Light, which he purchased from the local superette. She said, "Hi" and just looked at him, smiling a lovesmile, in awe of him and in love. She was now his dream, his dream woman and JD wanted to be with her. Then, figures of her parents and his parents appeared, since they looked the same, and it appeared to him that she had lived here a long time ago, which place would be known to him as the civilisation of Lymphis on his backyard, doing the gardening though to her it looked like they were killing someone as they bent down with their shovels. She was screaming and then smiling, then screaming and then smiling, back and forth. She said, after this, "I'm Sophie Silver; I'm in love with you." She ended up disappearing. But after that something happened to JD. He was put in hospital again. This time in Hamilton. But before that it seemed to him that his heart stopped beating so he made a special drink which he heard a voice say was the tree of life. It was banana, coffee, mango juice with apple juice, or whatever else was in the juice, as long as it was juice and chilli powder. It was to him the tree of life. As he was sitting in Hamilton hospital, inhaling a cigarette, he saw images of Cain, Abel and Satan, together with Adam and Eve making drinks while playing games of cards. They had to make the tree of life, or the tree of death, or the tree of knowledge. The materials were all there. Satan he thought made the tree of life, and became an immortal, and could not be killed, as it protected him and made people not want to kill him though he killed people as a serial killer, then after twelve years it had worn off and the townspeople came to murder him as they woke up from their sleep.

SOUL EJECTION AND HOLY CHALICE BREASTS

While he was picked up by the crisis team, he saw images of the world's population doing soul ejections, and the pickup point was the seat in front of him, so he could see all the souls ejecting. This was when Sophie Silver came into his head, and, hearing her voice, telling him to eject them from his body by her speaking numbers and him doing nothing, they were ejected and she also explained to him that he would have a hermaphrodite forehead because he had a woman's voice in his mind. A hermaphrodite forehead would be a forehead that would have two bumps on it, that curved inward and outward in the centre, and that would be symmetrical. Throughout his time in hospital he heard messages about him having Holy Chalice Breasts and looking like a female supermodel, and having astral eyes that glowed in the dark with a blue, astral light. He also saw images of Dragonball Z and Wall E, and would have the ability to become Wall E and a super sayan and also of Ultimate Weapon in Final Fantasy Seven, where he would have Ultimate Weapon eye shadow. Throughout all this, he saw dolphins. For, at home, he went cross eyed in the mirror, then sat down, then he saw eyes going back and forth on the back of his eye lids, for some reason unknown to him, probably a form of self hypnosis, and he saw dolphins swim into his mind from outside to within a halo. These he thought scanned the universe. So throughout his stay he was seeing dolphins swimming into his mind through the air. A process then came to him about him, since he scanned the universe with a dolphin scanning technique, which he thought was the first sight of Adam, a process about having dark space flame hair and moon pattern eye shadow and eye shadow of Jupiter's orbital pattern and other body properties that came from the scanning.

THE HOLY PRODUCTS OF PANDORA ARE MADNESS

"The holy products of Pandora." Pandora spoke to herself, in her madness and delirium, remembering that boy Jarrad Dickson, the madness of him, placed in psychiatric wards all over Nonia for his schizophrenia, but his body, how it changed! She was seeing what he saw, an upturned eye and the darkness of satan in a pyramid, and her hair was flaming in the mirror in front of her as she spoke to herself, and she went crosseyed in the mirror, doing what he called "eye chasm reading." The art of making a third eye. Remembering her days as a famous singer, actress and supermodel, she knew that this would change everything. She was becoming a schizophrenic. Would she attempt suicide to become an albino in heaven? For Jarrad believed his body had changed and he was constantly drawing patterns on his forehead to do a space time continuum plane shift; to teleport and time travel on the space time continuum. He attempted suicide off the Pa at Hahei to kill himself and go to heaven, for he thought that if he died, then in heaven he would wake up in a circle of flowers with pretty women around him, waiting to have sex with him and that he would be an albino. His greatest wish was to be an albino, and he wouldn't settle for anything less. She was seeing roses and hearing voices that told her that her body was changing, and she just heard a voice as she made four eyes by softening them saying that she would have rose window sclara. "Rose window sclara!" she thought. She was finding it hard to think, but she remembered seeing Jarrad on television and lusting for him; lusting for his personality, his body and his being. She would go to him and escape across the world. Bring him back to America, for that was his greatest dream also, to go to America. She knew he was currently not in a psychiatric ward but at home in Hahei, that holiday destination with thousands streaming along the beach in the summer. She would bring him to America and they would have sex. And be with each other; schizophrenic and schizophrenic. One day they would end up in the same psychiatric ward as each other. It did not matter to her, as long as they were with each other. She heard the voice of Michelle Mathew.

WORD STRESS DISORDERS AND THE SUICIDE DON'T TELL CLUB

She knew of one of his other greatest dreams. That is, his thoughts relating to his non-existent word stress disorder, where he thought he felt pain at the words "Don't tell" from the age of 16 to 20, where he had his first breakdown on the fateful day of the 18th of October. This was her 18th of October, though it was not as severe, and was similar more to the 18th of August, his second breakdown. But he thought that those with a word stress disorder are placed in a warehouse, and he thought that famous actresses were afflicted with them; and he thought that he too was going there and would be with them in that warehouse, with no bank account, discarded by society. That's what he thought, and he thought that she was there, having been afflicted by a suicide word stress disorder. For he thought he thought of suicide at the "don't" word and the "tell" word. "The holy products of Pandora are madness" she spoke out loud; this time screaming in front of the mirror as she saw her two eyes with a monobrow in a delusion. "It's time to leave Pandora, but first to Death Valley, for the Hollywood Walpurgis night." Pandora had read up on the life of Jarrad Dickson, and knew how obsessed he was with Faust by Goethe, and she felt in her delirium that there would be a Walpurgis Night at Death Valley, albeit a Hollywood one, with film characters, like there was that disaster at Hahei beach, or Hue beach in the mind of Jarrad, where the Sirians were over the top on their spaceship and aliens crashed and were haunted by ghosts of the village from the pa. And Pandora's People was constantly killing itself and releasing its soul endlessly on the Pa, which was going on in the mind of Jarrad.

JARRAD, DON'T KILL YOURSELF OVER ME

"Jarrad, don't kill yourself over me" lipping in front of the mirror, then moving to her suitcase which was packed even though she was in delirium.

THE BURNING ROSE

Roseblood this Valentines Day bled. A breeze swam blonde hair around the burning rose, blazing from a candle flame. The blonde hair belonged to a diva. The window was open in the apartment. A painting hang, old and ancient, saffron coloured and red. Two people were in it. One woman was holding a knife and tears fell from her eyes, she had just stabbed the man that she loved in the heart and then stabbed herself, weary from immortal age. The story of the painting was that the two were time travellers in the unverae dimension, and that the two, having lived for billions of years and having enough of life and love, decided to die together, and thus ended their lives. But they didn't die, and it was a gesturc they made, they were saying in the painting, "We know about you." It was the original. How it ended up in Nonia no one knew. It hung in an old, gold frame, with twirls around it and roses, blossoms and dandelions. A tear fell onto a rose thorn, as Pandora burned the rose given to her by her husband. She sat in an old chair, uncushioned and wooden, as she glanced outside the window. She was weary from her life as a star. A singer. A supermodel. An actress. She was about to lead a different life, but first she was faking a suicide attempt. She looked from the city view out of the window at the painting for tenderness, feeling their pain. They knew about her. About her pain. She was leaving her husband and beginning a life in the country. For faking her death she had a note, it went

To the Roseblood, my fans, and to my husband, goodbye. I have drowned myself in the sea.
The time has come for me to part with you. I'm at an end.
Goodbye,
Pandora

She had not packed her belongings. All she had was cash. She left the note on the night table for her husband to find and left. She was to begin a new life in the country, where she had a house. With one last look about the apartment, she left and walked out, unseen. Hidden.

A SHARED PSYCHOSIS

Pandora was wading through and made it to the outer edges of
the marsh and was in a desert, gold and flittering shadows
breaking past her and around her on the mountaintops. But all
around Nonia news came of her death and people were killing
themselves in mock attempts. They cut off their faces, their
noses; mouths, ears and eyes. They walked while cutting and
collected them in their bloody arms and hands to the valley of
death, and Pandora saw all the bodies lying down, dead,
around a small fountain, the fountain of Death, the only
source of water in the valley, and cried. She saw herself as the
source of all this pain. Others had killed themselves in their
bathtubs with a TV screen on, others in front of the TV
wearing goldrimmed glasses and silver suits. A homunculus
was growing in the fountain out of all the severed face parts,
and it was the shape of a heart. "Hello," it said, "My name is
Homunculus Cray, and I'll be your associate. The last master
I served was the God Faustus, who created twelve universes,
those before the primavera universe, which blocked the
collective unconscious before it, after what happened to the
Siriuses, who blocked it by expanses of dark space time.
Tonight you shall become an albino." And nearing her, out of
the fountain, he made gestures with his hands, making film
images with hand magic, and showed her what she'd have. He
continued speaking from out of the fountain, his red mouths
of feet slowly letting water drip onto the desert ground,
"You'll have the eyes of Horus." Such he said, and came by
her side. She was stunned into silence, but saw first the
beginnings of a white rose, a rose that would turn her into an
albino. A star star star albino rose, with star eyes albino
making her into. She motioned her hands around her eyes, and
her eyes had already changed. She felt a different bone
structure, a bone structure shaped like a four pointed star. She
moved towards the water, with Homunculus Cray beckoning
her, and saw in the water, Narcissus, his hair white and
flaming and golden eyes, the most golden coloured gold ever
seen, and her eyes changed colour to gold and she generated

the beauty equal to Narcissus, the beauty god who created universes. His image dissolved and staring back from the water was her reflection, full of beauty, and she had fame eyes, a fame mouth and a fame nose. And a catwalk smile. And star features. She was full of beauty.

MICHELLE MATHEW

Flaming orange, blonde and yellow hair like shooting stars came from the pale, milky white skin of Pandora, also known as Sophie Underwent as she hung in dark space. She was tall, skinny and white. She was an Arian. An Aryan. An Eleenzetrialeen. An Ulzat. A star star star star star star star rose white albino. A RoseumThornycee. A Zabuga. Right now she was in her total form, as she hovered in dark space before a huge moon, seeing its shadow as its sun was behind it. She heard voices, distant, of those dead; the voices of vampires. Softly floating in dark space, she was tall and white yet golden, the golden sheen of an Arian. Her golden eyes were blazing, and they were the gold of rose petal irises, irises with pictures of a rose, golden roses with eleven white pupils within the outer edges that were spun in circles. She had a fifty-five omega forehead, allowing a greater accentuation of her forehead, so small protrusions came out of it, and a perfect circle forehead. Which bore the mark of a perfect circle upon it. She was a white rose. She had fire hair, blazing up in flame shapes three times her body length. She had pointed ears, like the elves, and star constellation earrings of diamond, to store books and records, objects and spaceships. She had a star constellation of four five pointed shooting stars on her forehead that slowly moved around, never bumping into each other and she had a scanner adjustment system in between her eyes, which was a small diamond. She had a three fold inverted nose, with three parts to it, and inverted lips which curved like rose petals, red as a vampire's blood; she had coloured teeth and black, white and red coloured fingernails on eleven fingers on each hand. She had roses for nipples, and holy chalice breasts. She had an E perfect face and omega lips, that had black and white edges, that slowly curved around, revealing lip chasms. She had properties of the first great languages. She had a Sanskrit tongue, with sanskrit letters on it and Latin lips, with the word DICTUM and ancient Greek eyebrows, with ancient Greek letters on them. She was white, white, white and red, red, red and black, black, black. And gold. And blonde, orange and yellow.

THE HOLY GOTH

"There is no afterlife. Voices of vampires, a death cry of a chinalbino and the ecstasy of the sirens is what is heard when you approach a moon, hearing the voices of the dead from its shadow. The dead lie rotten and dissolved, but the living want immortality. Such is life. That is a moon's secret, my confidant." Michelle Mathew spoke to her son, The Holy Goth, named Michael Mathew. He is 800 years old and an immortal, and she spoke to him from his spaceship window, looking at a moon of Solaris, the black one. His spaceship is a pyramid of darkness, with a blotch of black in the middle, slowly fading its colour to see through along the edges, like a black cloud in a pyramid. Mathew sat in the darkness, in a hollowed square, beyond the window edge and sat up, moving towards his mother and was caught in the light of the Solaris, as it was dark in the viewing room. She saw him, as she had seen him countless times, his hair was black and flaming, rising in a perfect circle three times his body length; his eyes were rosebuds, still young, not old enough for roses, though they were opening; small white dots of eleven sat in a circle on the rosebud, and they spun around as he turned his sight towards his mother. He opened his inverted mouth, with omega lips that held a black omega symbol on the top lip and spoke, his pointed tongue shaping words. "But the living can't help but forsake their immortality, mother. Mathena Underwent, your greatest adversary, God, is somewhere out there, in the midst of a breakdown over the death of his wife Sophie Silver, that goddess, who came from the Arch Universe, far before this time, where Omega lived, and sorcerers and others of greatness, though with a Big Boom they vanished. He is the Holy Ghost, the Holy Church, the Holy Blood and the Holy Wood. I too have gone through the process of the Holy Wood. You can open it and start it whenever you want, and a mystical process it is. I am the Holy Wood. One day I too shall be Holy Church, Holy Ghost and Holy Blood. But only one can be Holy Water. I need to kill him to become Holy Water. I shall drink the water blood from his aura veins and breathe it in. I shall find him. The time is ripe for picking. We shall extend our empire across the universes, and beyond the outer reaches of space, to the non space realms and beyond, to the depths of forgotten, dead civilisations that lie out there beyond the borders. To the eagles as big as stars and the Eagle Mountain, bigger than this universe. We shall extend our empire. So we have goals, mother" he said, slowly drawling out 'mother', "To rule the cosmos, to kill Mathena and for me to become Holy Water and for us to ensure our immortality." Such he said, and Michelle held up her hand in her red robes and touched his cheek, white and albino, and said, "Before the moon you told me your secret, and it is love, my confidant." All this Jarrad Dickson was seeing as he sat at home, inhaling a cigarette, when all of a sudden, an actress walked onto his backyard, the actress Pandora. "Hello, I am Pandora, how are you Jarrad? I've come to be with you. I've spoken to the New Zealand government and I'd like to be with you in America, we can live together in the countryside. I too have been diagnosed with schizophrenia and I too have seen the darkness of Satan and the upturned eye of God."

TI AND DO

In the personal quarters of Ti and To black, flittering and evanescent shadows around a mirror danced as Ti and To applied their make-up for tonight's performance at Mathena's birthday party. They were whispering to each other, brother and sister, "No, he has to die," "No, she has to die," "No, Ti has to die," "No, To has to die" and together, "No, they...have...to...die!" Made up, before the mirror, their hair was frizzy; one black, the other white. Eye shadow crept up on each, around each other's eyes, slowly curving upwards and downwards beyond the edges, purple and pretty, with gold lines bordering it. Yin and Yang was the dress To wore, balanced with black and white shadow and light and the suit Ti wore was an Astral Eye, with aqua blue eyes spotted all along it. Dressed to kill, they finished applying their white and black make up. White make up for To, black for Ti. The holy stamp of Roseblood was on their foreheads, an image of a rose painted out of blood; ancient and ghastly. Ti and To, The Insider and The Outsider were obsessed with Roses and mystery. They chattered and sang in their apartment as they prepared for tonight's performance. All this Jarrad foresaw as he walked to the Pa with Pandora, and all of a sudden she disappeared from him and he was alone, and he looked down and saw the eye of Horus, and whoever sees the eye of Horus dies. He was scared and tired so lit a cigarette and went back down the Pa. It was not really Pandora or Sophie Silver, his shadow. But it was Pandora herself, his creation in Pandora's People. "Pandora the Arian," he thought, as he walked back home inhaling his third cigarette. Lately he had been concerned about Nonia and the novel he was writing, Song of Sillity of Might. He was an albino he thought again, as he dragged down the smoke. The smoke was relieving as it relaxed him and gave him something to do other than write. But it was not everything. He could kill himself. Become pure matter without consciousness, extending his lifetime in the universe for immortality. Planets and stars were all he was concerned with lately. "SHE HAS TO LIVE" he thought and "I", he thought, "OR HE HAS TO DIE."

THE SUPERMODEL CLONED HITLER

The supermodel cloned Hitler; then his head was cut off and taken to the second moon out of earth's orbit, then moved to another area of dark space. There his head was put on another body and he had his own civilisation. Then the supermodel returned to destroy Hitler and his civilisation; she then burned it down with flames.

A TRANSFORMATION INTO AN ARYAN

She was an Aryan, and an Arian. She was of the Aryan race, with golden eyes, and high, waving flame hair. She could fly in outerspace, across moons and planets and stars, through black holes stretching her body. She had milky white albino skin of a new type of Arian. This is what JD saw as he sat on the couch. Then, hearing a voice calling him to go to the mirror he walked down the hallway.

EYE CHASM READING

He then heard a voice telling him to go cross eyed and did, and his eyes became three in the mirror, "Move it left, that's right, then right, then up, up and down," he heard and did what the voice told him to do. In around two minutes he managed to put an eye into his forehead and his pupils enlarged, covering the entire iris. He then moved into bed. He thought the supermodel had returned from outerspace after destroying Hitler to see him, as he thought that she was in love with him. As he was in bed, he saw eyes in the wall, his own eye, and a pyramid of darkness in the corner and a blue, white and black eye above the doorway. Surely this was the darkness of Satan and the cloning light of God, he thought. In bed, he got three erections over the supermodel and then, in the morning, having stayed up all night, he slowly got up out of bed, hearing a voice, and put his slippers on and some clothes, then walked out, following what the voice said, as he was new to hearing voices and was not sure who it was that was talking to him. He walked to the bridge to meet the tall, flaming haired supermodel but she wasn't there, then walked to the cemetery to find a secret base that also wasn't there, then sat in the toilets awaiting someone that would transfer his body to another dimension with a civilisation called Lymphis, as the older one that was around him had been destroyed and everyone had been cloned, or so he thought. Cloning was the issue in his mind at the time. Walking to the waterfront, he was confronted by the image of a man with another man that was trying to stab him in the heart, or the man was trying to persuade the other man to do it, but he wouldn't.

MICHAEL AND MATHEW

So JD walked to the waterfront, and then was confronted with a financier named Michael who ate brains and hearts of dead children and wanted to clone his brain for his IQ points underneath his old school, and who wanted to also be an Aryan and an Arian, for JD thought that he had become an Aryan also, but did not necessarily believe it, for he had not had that much time to think about it. "Go to the emergency room," the voice said before when he was near the hospital, and he nearly did, but not before realizing it would get him put back into a mental health ward as it had on the 18th of October 2007, where he checked himself into hospital thinking he would have a heart attack. So here he was, on the waterfront of Auckland harbour, when a lawyer named Mathew came to see him, who looked like the financier and was his twin brother, and was talking to him about the legal restraints of being cloned, and then two other figures arrived talking to him about being cloned and signing a contract that they held but was invisible. They then walked off and JD followed the main road of Queen street up until he saw his father and events transpired and he was put back into hospital. This was when he thought that aliens had crashed and they were waiting for him in Albert Park, near the university.

Chapter 8

A hand passed through blonde hair of a goddess, through its supermodel hair gloss and over her Holy Chalice Breasts in a velvet red gown, and down further to Hell as the Heaven eyes stared closer at him, God; looking she saw into rose windows of eyes, and fire hair of black, and seeing shooting stars on his forehead and she kissed him then, laying her red lips on his Omega and Alpha two lips, inverted lips, and kissed his nose, that was threefold and inverted also, and she moved away from him then and went to the bed of the Unverae dimensional castle, for they were in the bedroom, and sat on the bed. She said "Come here, little rose, little rose, little rose red, my Michael Mathew." And he moved over to her, and undressed her from her red gown and she undressed him from his suit, and they lay naked in bed kissing and touching, then had sex with rose flowers touching, and their hair was flaming as they did the act, moving upwards, and this was Michael Mathew and Heather Marks in love. He had finally met with Pandora.

"The holy products of Pandora, are madness, its all in the mind," Rose, Pandora, spoke, moving her red dress onto her again and leaving the bed a mess. "Soon we shall die, me, Rose and Sophie, that Hua Nian, or other name, Rose Blood and we shall insert ourselves into your face; I shall live in your lips. Rose in your rosy cheeks and Rose in your eyes, that's where our minds shall be and we shall be immortal with you. Only God is a true immortal, though we posses long life spans we cannot live forever, only you can. The parallel worlds have been melded together. I am Pandora, and I opened Pandora's box. I am your source, your Arian bride, my dear. Death becomes you…"

Become an immortal in death. Death is immortality. We don't seek death, we seek immortality. Beyond the pale is immortality; roses are red, death is black and immortality is black too. We are heading towards the life of God. May we be happy in death.

"Sweet Pandora, how lovely you are," Jarrad said.

www.ingramcontent.com/pod-product-compliance
Lightning Source LLC
Chambersburg PA
CBHW031216270326
41931CB00006B/580